Don't Quit Your Day Job, Learn To Love It

iUniverse, Inc.
New York   Bloomington

Don't Quit Your Day Job, Learn To Love It

iUniverse books may be ordered through booksellers or by contacting:

iUniverse
1663 Liberty Drive
Bloomington, IN 47403
www.iuniverse.com
1-800-Authors (1-800-288-4677)

Because of the dynamic nature of the Internet, any Web addresses or links contained in this book may have changed since publication and may no longer be valid. The views expressed in this work are solely those of the author and do not necessarily reflect the views of the publisher, and the publisher hereby disclaims any responsibility for them.

ISBN: 978-1-4401-5285-6 (pbk)
ISBN: 978-1-4401-5288-7 (cloth)
ISBN: 978-1-4401-5287-0 (ebk)

Library of Congress Control Number: 2009931028

Printed in the United States of America

iUniverse rev. date: 7/29/2009

Don't Quit Your Day Job, Learn To Love It

Carrie Nelson

Table of Contents

Preface

I have always wanted to help employees to be happier and more successful. We spend a lot of time at work and should truly enjoy the process. We should get a sense of pride and fulfillment from the tasks we accomplish each day. We should also look forward to our future and plan for greater levels of success. That way we are enjoying both the journey and the destination.

Many companies try to help employees to be more successful by spending money on development and training programs. However, these programs typically focus on only one area of employee development at a time and are set up classroom-style in a public forum. This is not always successful because it does not allow for quiet reflection of the material or for the individual to personalize the information to their specific situation.

So, I wrote this book because I wanted to provide all of the tips and tools needed for any employee to navigate through their unique work environment. It includes information on traditional training topics, like time management and organizational skills. However, it also provides information on non-traditional topics that most companies do not focus on when training employees, like how to handle stress, how to manage a boss's expectations, and how to have work/life balance.

How come no one has thought of this before? There are two schools of thought in the field of workplace practices: researchers and practitioners. The researchers are typically professors who know all of the theories and conduct research studies, mainly on college campuses. The practitioners are the ones who apply the theories in the field and work for various companies as business consultants or human resource managers.

I have had the opportunity to work in both fields so I am able to bridge the gap between the two. While pursuing my Ph.D. in

Industrial-Organizational Psychology, my research focused on team-work, judgment and decision making, and the testing and assessment of employees. This included understanding complex psychological theories that motivates people at work, both as individuals and as team mates. I have also served as an Adjunct Professor to a number of different universities and have been able to share feedback on these topics with both traditional and adult learners.

Understanding the theories is only the beginning though, it is important to be able to apply them. In my corporate career, I have served as an employee, consultant, and trainer to over 25 different companies around the world. I have been involved in both start-up environments and international conglomerates. After working in so many diverse environments, I noticed a lot of similarities in the mistakes employees tend to make and roadblocks they find difficult to overcome.

Many of the problems can be easily fixed, but it takes hard work and dedication from each individual employee. This book was designed to focus on these major topics that employees struggle with. Throughout the book, I pose questions to the reader in order to give them a chance to critically review their work environment and I challenge them to make things better. I also developed several mini-assessments, specifically for this book. The assessments are intended to engage the reader to learn more about themselves and to understand how they can be more successful in their job.

Throughout the writing of the book, I also conducted job satisfaction surveys with both employees and employers, to get their feedback about various situations and what they wanted to see changed at their workplace. By combining all of this information into one comprehensive document, the ultimate goal is to help people achieve even more success at work. *Anyone can learn to love their job and this book will show you how.*

Ch. 1 – Assess Your Situation

So often time it happens, we all live our life in chains, and we never even know we have the key. --The Eagles, "Already Gone"

We all have the power to transform our lives. Each and every one of us can be and should be living the life that we were destined for. We should lead a purpose driven life, feel good about what we do at work, and feel useful and productive. We work on average 2,000 hours every year and should not just expect a paycheck in return. We should also feel satisfied and content that the work we do matters and that it makes a difference in people's lives. Why do so many people feel unhappy about their jobs? Why do we get stuck in a rut and can't seem to progress to the next level? Why do we feel exhausted at the end of the day? Why is it so hard to work with other people? What does our boss really want from us? How can we get all of our tasks and responsibilities done so that we can have enough time left at the end of the day to enjoy ourselves? These questions are addressed in this book.

In today's crazy world, we all have to juggle multiple tasks. We have to keep ourselves organized and focused on our work while getting along with our co-workers, making our boss happy, and having enough time in the day to focus on our personal lives too. It is enough to drive anyone mad. Do you often feel stressed out? Do you avoid certain people at work because they drive you crazy? Do you dread going to meetings or performing certain tasks? Do you ever feel overwhelmed and do not look forward to the future? If you are feeling this way then isn't it worth it to focus some time and energy on making changes for the better? There are things you can do to make your job more fulfilling and to combat the negativity that can surround you at work. First you must recognize what is driving you crazy and making you unhappy in our job. Once you target the problem, you can begin looking for potential solutions that fit your unique situation. *Your work life can be better.* It will just take some hard work from you. Are you ready?

What Is Making You Unhappy?

First let's take a deep breath and step back from the situation to examine your complete work environment. Before you can do anything to make your life better, you need to have a calm and centered mind. You are about to embark on a journey to make every aspect of your work life better. It is to your advantage to focus exclusively on the following tasks without distractions.

What are the top five things that cause you worry, sleeplessness, or just makes you hate your job? What kinds of things have been on your mind about work in the last few weeks? Is there a certain person who annoys you or makes you feel bad? Are there certain tasks that you do not like to perform? Do you dread the upcoming performance evaluation process at work? Do you hate attending certain meetings? Or are you stressed about tight deadlines? Maybe the problem is less specific and has to do with uninteresting work or possibly lacking the chance to advance up the corporate ladder?

List the top five things that are causing you to be unhappy at work:

1.

2.

3.

4.

5.

Why Are These Things Making You Unhappy?

Did you do the exercise above? This isn't going to work unless you are willing to put some effort into it. Done now? Great. Now let's look at each of these issues further. What are some of the underlying problems? You listed *what* the problem is, the next step is to evaluate *why* it is causing you grief. Spend time thinking about each problem individually and how you feel in that situation. Is it the person, place, process, or some other factor that is causing the discomfort? For example, do you hate Ryan because he always asks the same questions and you feel like you are doing part of his job for him? Or do you hate Jen because you feel she is rude and condescending? Do you hate going to meetings because they are long and boring or because you have to speak and you are shy? Let's get into the heart of the matter and unload your feelings about these issues.

Write 2-3 sentences about why each item above is causing you to be unhappy:

1.

2.

3.

4.

5.

Doesn't it feel better just to vent? By compiling your major issues or stressors into one document, you can get a clearer idea of what may be wrong and we can begin making plans for improvement. This book is about facing problems and fixing them. We are going to conduct an assessment of your entire environment. The goal is to locate other potential problems or stressors so that they can be addressed and fixed. We will also look at ways you can have more fun at work and feel more fulfilled.

Many people don't know what is triggering their unhappiness. Often they walk around miserable for days, weeks, or even years without really thinking about what is causing them to feel this way. However, once you know the cause, you can try to work toward a solution. No matter what the problem is, you can do things to make improvements and feel better every day. To be honest, it is not even that hard to make immediate changes in your work life. There are no secret or advanced formulas. It just takes time and dedication on your part. Are you ready to make that commitment?

Just imagine how you will feel when you have conquered all of the major obstacles in your job. You will have more time and energy and feel less stress every day. You will have a clear path toward your future work goals and will be able to celebrate each milestone that you achieve. You will have an open relationship with your boss and will work together to make each other successful. You will also have good working relationships with your co-workers and be able to help them achieve their goals too. Perhaps most importantly, when your career is on track, your personal life will improve because you will have more time and positive energy to focus on the things that matter most.

In The Moment

Evaluate the top five lists that you created earlier. Do you notice any similar themes throughout the lists? If you dislike a certain person, what happens when they come around? Do you feel upset and anxious and get ready to lash out before they even have a chance to open their mouth? Or do you get nervous at a certain meeting and have anxiety before it even starts? Often just the anticipation of the problem can cause more wasted time and effort than the actual problem itself. If you feel this way and are nervous with anticipation, take a step back and breathe. Take a walk, talk to a friend, or get some exercise. Remove yourself from the situation for a moment. Then you can look at the situation more objectively and determine what is causing the problem and how you are going to respond. Then, make sure to *respond* and not *react*. By responding, you are more in control of the situation.

Learn how to read the signs of when you are getting upset so that you will know when to stop it. Some people can feel a nervous tension in their stomach whereas others might literally feel hot under the collar. Some may feel sweaty palms where others have an increased heart rate. Almost any kind of body aches and pains can be associated with nervous tension. Sometimes it builds up over a day, a week, or even over a lifetime. It is important to pay attention to what your body is trying to tell you and take a more proactive standpoint to try and fix the problem before it gets out of hand. Once a major problem presents itself, it is important to respond to it immediately to get it resolved, but also to make contingency plans so that it won't happen again.

Take Control And Stay Positive

How much control do you have over your negative feelings, your tension, and your stress level? How you view any event has a lot to do with how you feel about it and the resulting anxiety. Negative thinking patterns can distort your view of what is really going on in your life. These thoughts can make you feel depressed, worried, stressed out, or even provoke you into making poor choices. For example, if you have anxiety about getting negative feedback from your boss, you might be tense before they start every meeting with you. Your anxiety might start hours before their visit and when they finally arrive, you might be so tense that you are not thinking clearly or acting as professional as you normally do. If things like this happen, it shows a lack of control over your own negative feelings and emotions.

Learning to take a positive view of life and of yourself can have major rewards and also allows you to take back control. It can increase your happiness, your productivity, and ultimately lead to a better reputation and career. There is a clear link between having a positive outlook and the resulting health benefits. People who maintain a calm and positive demeanor have better coping skills in general and experience less depression and anxiety, have better immunity to colds and flues, and they have fewer physical problems. Imagine that you can control the way you feel and even reduce some of the health issues you may be having, all by thinking more calmly and positively!

Quick tips on maintaining a calm demeanor:

- ✓ Learn relaxation techniques such as deep breathing and yoga

- ✓ Eat healthy food and stay away from excessive caffeine and alcohol

- ✓ Exercise regularly, even a brisk walk can do wonders for how you feel

- ✓ Practice confronting your fears and embracing change

- ✓ Build on your communication skills to express your problems

- ✓ Don't be afraid to ask others for help when you need it

Clean Your Glasses

Many people do not have a realistic or positive view of themselves or others. This causes them to focus and dwell on the negative aspects of every day occurrences, rather than on the joy and fulfillment. This can lead to a giant negative path to no where. For example, some people are very self critical and scold themselves for the slightest mistake. Others are very critical of the people around them and are quick to point out errors or place blame. Some people just walk through life with general feelings of negativity where they discount the positive aspects of life and expect failure as the likely outcome. For people who think this way, failure is typically the result. These kinds of thoughts and feelings can keep people from achieving their full potential and having good relationships with others. It is a self fulfilling prophecy. However, there is a way to turn this around.

Before you really start this journey of improving your work life, take a look around at your physical environment and determine if you are fostering a happy and positive work environment or a negative and unhealthy one. Anyone can become a more positive person who spreads joy and love to themselves and others, rather than negativity and anger.

The important first step is to recognize any negative thoughts you have and turn them around into more positive hopes and dreams. It sounds easy to put on paper but a lot more difficult to do and to train your self over time.

Take a look at your work space. Is it clean and orderly? Or is it cluttered and uninviting? Can you find everything you need? Or do you often have to hunt around for things? Do you have pictures of family and friends? Or is it stark and bare? Do you have awards displayed or gifts that co-workers have given you? Or do you have used wrappers, old papers, and unopened mail? Some people find funny jokes and tape them to their computer or cubicle to give others a laugh. Take a look at those. Are they positive sayings that are meant to uplift the reader or are they negative sayings that poke fun at misfortune? If there are negative statements, even if they appear to be funny, take them down and replace them with something more inspiring. You can even make it a fun task each week or month to find a new one to post. Here are a few examples of inspirational messages you could post around your workspace:

- "What would you attempt to do if you knew you could not fail?"

- "Work like you don't need the money, love like you've never been hurt, and dance like no one is watching"

- "The three essentials of happiness are something to do, something to love, and something to hope for"

- Or use any of the quotes at the beginning of the chapters in this book

Once your physical environment is cleaned up, think about the way you act toward others at work and the things you say. When someone says good morning, do you respond back with a smile and a positive greeting or do you say, "it looks like it is going to rain." Maybe instead you immediately start to tell them about your personal problems or your workload or maybe even gossip about someone in the office. Even worse than this are the people who do not answer back at all when someone says good morning to them. We will review these topics later in the book, about how to project a positive demeanor and to brighten the day of others. However, start thinking about these things now so that you can start coming up with new ideas on how to handle these situations. Of course we will also review what to do about the grumpy people and how to try and snap them out of their funk. We are all in this together and should work as a team to help and support each other, and to have as much fun doing it as possible.

Take Time

No matter how you spend your day, make sure to use your breaks wisely. If you have a break, spend it on something you enjoy. Have lunch with a friend who has a positive attitude. Seek out a new employee and help them get acclimated. Do not spend break time complaining about what you don't like. If that is what you normally do, make an effort to change that bad habit and encourage your co-workers to do the same. People fuel each other with their attitudes. You can spread seeds to make things grow or spread garbage and let things fester and rot. Which way would you rather live? As you turn things around in your own work life and begin living more positive and upbeat, track how many improvements you see. As you build momentum, you will see more and more good things happening around you. You must always take time to step back from the situation so that you can see it objectively and so that you can take time to smell the roses and acknowledge and celebrate your achievements at work.

Overall Job Satisfaction Assessment

There are mini assessments throughout this entire book. This is an important part of the journey because you must know who you are before you can fully understand what you want and need from your job and career. The first assessment is about overall job satisfaction. This will give you a brief overview of the strengths and weaknesses in your environment. Don't be afraid to be honest. You don't have to share your answers with anyone else if you don't want to. It will also help you see where you need to focus as you go through the rest of this book.

On a scale of 1-5 with 5 being the best, rate the following statements based on your current job situation. The scale below can be used to help you in determining your scores.

1 – Never
2 – A few times a year
3 – Once a month
4 – At least once a week
5 – Typically every day

Organizational Skills

_____ My work space is neat and orderly

_____ I always complete my work assignments on time

_____ I consistently maintain "To Do" Lists

_____ I typically show up to meetings on time

_____ I am able to stay focused on my job without being interrupted

_____ Total Score for Organizational Skills

Goal Setting

_____ My job description is clear to me

_____ I know my own strengths and weaknesses

_____ I have written work goals for the next 6 or 12 months and I review them regularly

_____ I am enthusiastic about my future career and have a plan to achieve higher levels of success

_____ I celebrate when I finish a project, achieve a goal, or complete a milestone

_____ Total Score for Goal Setting

Attitude

_____ I look forward to going to work in the morning

_____ I feel good throughout the day

_____ I am proud to work for this company

_____ Most interactions at work are positive

_____ I have fun at work

_____ Total Score for Attitude

Communication

_____ I can speak at ease with anyone at work

_____ My written communications are concise, to the point, and easy to understand

_____ The meetings I attend are useful and I am able to contribute to them as needed

_____ I demonstrate active listening skills in all of my verbal interactions with people

_____ I am confident in giving presentations

_____ Total Score for Communication

Relationship with Boss

_____ I understand what motivates my boss and his/her work style preferences

_____ My boss knows what projects I am working on and how I typically spend my day

_____ My boss keeps me informed of things I need to know

_____ My boss lets me do my job without interfering

_____ My boss is helping me to progress in my career

_____ Total Score for Relationship with Boss

Relationships with Co-Workers

_____ My relationships with my co-workers are friendly

_____ I treat others the way they want to be treated

_____ I help co-workers when they need it and do not expect anything in return

_____ I am tolerant of other viewpoints even if I do not necessarily agree with them

_____ If I have a disagreement with a co-worker, I am able to easily forget it and move on

_____ Total Score for Relationships with Co-Workers

Stress

_____ I know immediately when I am feeling physical or psychological symptoms of stress

_____ I know what situations tend to stress me out and I have strategies to deal with it proactively

_____ I am generally stress free and people or situations at work do not affect my stress level

_____ I generally eat healthy and exercise in order to keep my stress level low

_____ I try to incorporate humor into my work day

_____ Total Score for Stress

Work/Life Balance

_____ I typically work my scheduled hours and do not need to put in overtime

_____ I have good control over my schedule and where I spend my time

_____ I have enough energy at the end of the day to take care of myself and others when I get home

_____ My job never interferes with time I spend with my family and friends

_____ I have enough "me" time to recharge my batteries as needed

_____ Total Score for Work/Life Balance

_____ Grand Total

The assessments in this book do not have a scoring key because there is no ideal answer and you are not expected to be perfect. So, simply count your points based on each score and see how you did. It is important to look at how you scored in each individual category to see where the strengths and weaknesses are in your environment. If you scored high in a certain category, you can become a champion in your office for this skill set and mentor others. For example, if you scored high in attitude, turn yourself into a superhero of positive attitude at work so that you can spread that joy to others. Give yourself daily or weekly goals for spreading your positive energy to others and give yourself small rewards each time you make someone feel good. For the categories where you scored the lowest, you may want to pay particular attention to those chapters in this book. Make a commitment to yourself right now to make improvements in those areas so that you can really enhance your work life. Everyone has strengths and weaknesses and it is our individual differences that contribute to the success of the team as a whole. Try taking this survey periodically to see how you are doing at any given time.

Conclusion

The purpose of this chapter was to evaluate your complete work situation. We reviewed the top five things that are making you unhappy and we delved into the reasons of why these things have control over your happiness. We also discussed how you can take back control over how you feel, how you think, and how you spend your time. It is important to be calm and centered so that you can look at your situation objectively and be able to make active changes to improve the quality of your life. The assessment here was meant to get you more in tune with your strengths and areas that need improvement in your work life. Now that you know what areas you need to focus on, get ready to take control of your life and become a happier, more self-aware, and more productive employee.

The following chapters will walk you through the most important skills and proficiencies that every employee should continually work on developing. Topics are covered on getting organized, planning ahead and setting goals, having a positive attitude, and communicating effectively. Other chapters focus on building and maintaining good relationships with your boss and co-workers. Later chapters focus on handling stress and maintaining work/life balance. In order to help you be successful, there are several examples listed and tips that you can incorporate into your work day right now. There are also additional assessments so that you can further understand the qualities you have already and the potential qualities you may seek to develop. In order to be successful, you must be willing to make active changes in the way you perform tasks and the way you interact with people. It will require constant examination about yourself and your work environment along with thoughtful attention about your attitude and behavior. You may not be able to change everything in your environment, but you can change the way you think about it and how you react to various situations.

It may sound like a lot of work but the rewards are well worth it. By implementing a few small changes, you can enhance the quality of your work life and become a happier, more productive, and more successful employee. This can reduce your stress load, enhance the relationships you have with people at work, and help you to build a professional reputation. This will not only make you feel better everyday but it can also increase your job security and future growth potential. Who does not want that? So, are you ready? Let's go! The first thing to do is to get organized, both physically and mentally. We will review that topic in the next chapter.

Ch. 2 – Get Organized

Opportunity is missed by most people because it is dressed in overalls and looks like work. --Thomas Edison

Have you ever missed a great opportunity and then kicked yourself over it? Maybe opportunities passed you by while you were focused on other things? How confident are you that you have spent your time and attention at work on the kinds of tasks that will promote your career in the future? Are you performing the job that you were hired to do or do you typically get thrown various "miscellaneous" projects? In order to answer these questions more easily in the future, you must first get organized. Being organized will allow you to take more control over your day-to-day work activities and ultimately put you in charge of your career.

Getting organized is an important first step toward transforming your work life. You must get your environment organized before you can progress toward making other improvements like setting goals and enhancing the relationships you have with others. Being organized and having a professional image is important because the way you present yourself to others shows how much respect you have for yourself and for them. For example, how would it look if you came to work late, without taking a shower, without wearing professional clothes, and you ate breakfast at your desk while crumpling up the paper and shooting baskets into the garbage?

Everyone varies in their organizational skills. Most people do not live on either end of the spectrum from "neat freak" to "sloppy joe." You are probably more in the middle and have enough of a balance to get by and find things when you need them, but you can always try to make improvements to be even better. For example, you could improve the orderliness of your physical environment so that you could find things faster and easier. You could also make some simple changes to the way you maintain your schedule so that you are always on time for meetings and you never miss important events. These are topics that are discussed further in this chapter.

Some people have problems with procrastination whereas others can never say "no" to requests even if they are unreasonable. Sometimes we try to do it all ourselves without getting help from anyone and often we just get burnt out in the process. There is no easy formula for everyone to follow in every situation. We all need to learn how to adapt to the changing needs of our work life and be flexible enough to accommodate the important items on our schedules. This takes careful planning and forethought. It is not always easy but it is an important part of being a fully engaged employee with bright future career potential.

Problems With Disorganization

Being disorganized can negatively affect every aspect of a career. It can sully a reputation because someone who is disorganized can appear lazy, slow, dim-witted, uncaring, and untrustworthy. If you were the owner of your company, would you give a promotion to someone who shows up late, misses meetings, and loses work assignments? Probably not. People who are disorganized can be easily distracted and forgetful. They often procrastinate and focus on tasks that are more comfortable and easy to do. However, this is just plain laziness and will not contribute to job fulfillment or a successful career.

Being disorganized can also make people feel stressed out and can ultimately affect their overall health. We all get frazzled at one time or another and when that happens, we lose sight of what is happening around us. For example, if we are running late on a project and frantically searching our desk for a report that we lost, we are not focusing on other projects that are also due or the people around us who may need our attention. If this kind of situation happens often then our work relationships will suffer as a result. Then we just end up spending too much time absorbed in fixing the problems, when we could be accomplishing other tasks.

Do any of the following situations sound familiar?

- You can't find things and often spend time looking for them

- You are late to appointments because you are getting ready

- You have trouble keeping track of more than one project at a time

- Your co-workers get frustrated with you because you can't answer questions right away

- You sometimes go off on tangents while speaking to people

- You often spend time fixing unanticipated problems

- You feel stressed out because of deadlines

- You lose out on fun activities or time with family/friends because you spend too much time at work

We all have problems being organized from time to time. It can be difficult to keep track of everything that is going on in our lives and to keep our space neat and orderly. However, getting organized is one of the most important things we can do because it gives us more time to focus on important tasks. If we wallow in disorganization then the problem only snow balls and gets worse. This creates a never ending cycle of disaster. The worst part is that most people think they need more time. This is not true! It is not about working *longer* but about worker *smarter*. Often people waste a lot of time being disorganized but with some careful planning up front, we can save a lot of time, energy, and heartache later on.

Benefits Of Being Organized

By getting organized and learning to plan ahead consistently, you can get more work done in a shorter time frame. This will reduce your stress level and make you more successful at work. Being organized is not only good for you and your image, but it also allows others to work with you more easily. For example, if your work space is organized, you will appear to be more approachable by others. You will also appear to be more in control and able to handle responsibility. Additionally, if you are absent from work then others should be able to find any urgent items they may need from your work area. Here are some other benefits of being organized:

- It helps you to be prepared for both expected and unexpected problems

- It helps you save time for more important activities (ten minutes of planning can save you hours of time spent running around in circles or repairing the damage of unplanned activity)

- It provides a timetable for accomplishment and allows you to recognize and celebrate any milestones that you have achieved

- It provides a specific procedure for making decisions more quickly and moving forward on tasks

- It allows different departments to coordinate the efforts of many people so that shared goals can be accomplished with less time wasted

- It develops your vision of the future, by challenging you to define and identify what your ultimate career goals are and to pursue them

When you are organized, you save time looking for things, shopping for replacements, making excuses to others, and you improve your overall efficiency. You also look and feel better and portray a more professional attitude and demeanor at work. This can only be good for your career. You will save the company money because you won't order multiple supplies that you have lost or waste time looking for misplaced items. You will have a clear plan of action for each major project and be able to make decisions based on your long-term career goals.

You will be more in control of your schedule, know where you need to be and when, and you will ultimately get more work done.

Organizational Skills Assessment

Each person is unique and may require different levels and types of organizational skills at different points in their careers. For example, accountants are very busy during tax season and may not have time to make future plans or review their career goals during these months. However, when tax season is over, they might want to take stock of their previous accomplishments and take time to make plans moving forward. Everyone needs different organizational skills at different times.

The assessment below is for you to understand your level of organization at the current time. There are no right or wrong answers because everyone is different. ***Simply use this as a check-off list and mark the corresponding answer. How often do you spend time on the following activities?***

How often do you …	Daily	Weekly	Monthly	Quarterly	Annually	Never
Clean your work space?						
Delete old email?						
Review/ update your job description?						
Review written work goals?						
Make "To Do" Lists?						
Provide status reports to your boss?						

Dedicate specific time to focus on important projects?						
Take time to recharge your batteries?						

As with most things in life, there is no exact formula that works in every situation. What may be right for one person may not be right for another. However, you should spend enough time with planning and organizing each day and each major work assignment so that your tasks can be performed easily and so that your deadlines are met. You need to do the right amount of planning and organizing that is required by your job at any given moment. By seeing these tasks listed together, you may get some ideas on improvements you can make right away. Each topic will also be explored further in the following sections of this chapter.

Work Space

Your work space says a lot about your personality. Is it bright and welcoming or is it harried and disorganized? Do you have recent pictures of family or friends at happy events? Do you have art work that your children created? In your work space, you should have some private items to make it personalized such as family pictures, mementos, and perhaps some gifts that co-workers have given you. After you look at the aesthetics, which is typically the fun part, look at the usefulness and practicality of the space. Do you have enough room to sit comfortably? Is your keyboard and chair at an appropriate height? Can you reach all of the major tools you use without straining yourself? Do you have small items sorted, like pens, paper clips, paper, and files? When other people come to visit, is there a place for them to sit? What is the message that you are sending to others about yourself?

Think about your work space like a public relations campaign about who you are and where your career is leading to. Look around your work space as if you were seeing it for the first time. Walk around and look at it from different angles. What would someone think if they entered your work area for the first time? Take an inventory and determine if you really need everything. Does it all need to be there? Make solid plans to clean your workspace and do it in a timeframe that you are most comfortable. For example, plan to stay late one night and do it all at once or segregate ten minutes per day to clean up one area or drawer at a time. You should completely remove everything from each area, give it a good cleaning, and then return only the items that you need. For the items that you do not use, you can return them to the supply cabinet, file them away, or throw them out. You will be amazed by how much better you will feel when your work space is clean and orderly. You can have fun with this and put all of the garbage into bags and weigh it to see how many pounds your office is losing. You could even have a contest to reward people for losing the most pounds.

After your physical space is cleaned up, make sure to do the same thing with your electronic files. Many people wait too long before cleaning up email. Make sure to delete items you do not need or make files and sort items you may need later on. At least once a year go through all of your Word and Excel documents to make sure they are sorted in the appropriate online folder or if they can be deleted to make space for more important items. Your online calendar should be cleaned up and you should use it often. You should also maintain an electronic contact list and make sure it is updated. Having your contacts stored electronically also makes it easier to send email and stay in touch with important people.

As you clean out items, make a commitment to keep each area clean. It is actually pretty easy to clean up your work space. The hard part is in keeping it clean over time. If you are stubborn, you may want to focus on one small area at a time and make a three month commitment to keeping it clean. After the three months, you will be accustomed to keeping it clean and you can move on to another area in your work space to clean up. If you are inpatient like me, you will want to get it done all at once. Everyone is different and needs to do this at a pace that is comfortable. Either way, make sure to give yourself rewards for each milestone that you achieve. You should appreciate and celebrate your hard work. You should also have pride in your work space and want to keep it clean. Notice how much easier it is to find things. You may also notice that you feel better and can breathe easier because less stuff means less dust. If you are having trouble getting rid of items, you can type up that saying and tape it to your computer for motivation: "less stuff means less dust."

Operator's Manual

Think about your workflow and the way you perform each task. Do you have documented procedures on how to conduct operations? This means having clear written directions on how to perform each task. Having this kind of operator's manual can help to make sure you are conducting tasks efficiently and it can serve as a checks and balances to make sure nothing is missed. Additionally, an operator's manual can help if you are out of the office or if you need to train someone new, perhaps as you progress upward in the company. This may seem like a large undertaking but virtually every position can have an operator's manual. For example, a receptionist can have a manual for how to answer the phones and how to transfer calls. The manual can serve as a reference tool for tasks that are not performed often or for cross-training multiple employees. This can work in any position and for any level of the organization. For example, if you are a vice president, you might have a manual about the reports you expect from your staff and how they should be formatted along with the regular ongoing meetings you attend each week or month.

Creating an operator's manual typically takes time and requires the assistance of your boss and maybe some co-workers. It is a great exercise for different employees in a particular department to do together. You begin the process by breaking down your job into its basic components. For example, if you work in sales and a large part of your job is processing sales applications, then you would list each step in the process from taking the call, gathering information, checking credit, and obtaining a deposit. It is easiest to do this as you are actually performing the tasks so that you don't leave anything out. Once you have each step typed up into one document, make sure that the directions are clear. Imagine if you were a new employee with the company, would you still understand the directions? It helps to spell out each item rather than using acronyms. It also helps if you explain where to find tools and locate electronic documents. When you are finished, you can try asking someone in another department to review it so see if they can fully understand it. Having a complete operator's manual is an invaluable tool for when you want to train someone new. It also helps for when you are on vacation or out sick because it allows your co-workers and possibly your boss to chip in more and assist with your assignments so that your work will not pile up while you are out.

As part of the operator's manual, you might want to create a "decision matrix" also, depending on your job. A decision matrix includes a list of people who need to give "approval" before certain transactions occur and another list of people who need to be "informed" about certain transactions. For example, if you work in the human resource department and you process background checks during the recruiting process, you could make a list of each possible outcome and create directions about how to proceed. Perhaps that means there are cut-off scores for credit ratings whereby someone with credit of 500+ can be hired without approval, but if they score between 400-500 then they can not be hired unless it is approved by a division vice president, and anyone who scores below 400 can not be hired at all. Then you must also include a list of people who need to be informed each time someone is hired. So after each person passes the credit check, you might send an email to certain managers to inform them about the new employee who will be starting soon. Having all of this clearly listed in an operator's manual makes the entire work process run more smoothly. It allows everyone to see and agree upon the plan of action and allows for the decision making process to happen much more quickly.

To-Do Lists

Having an operator's manual is just the backbone of creating a successful work environment. Each work day presents unique situations and challenges that we need to track and resolve. Because of this, it is important to maintain To-Do lists of items we need to tackle and status reports of items we have completed. This allows us to know where we are going so that we can plan ahead, but it also allows us to recognize and celebrate the milestones we have achieved.

Maintaining a To-Do list is as simple as creating a list of everything you need to do, sometimes in order of priority, and keeping it with you so that you don't forget anything. You can have fun with it and color code the important tasks or give them letter grades of A through F. Having a complete list in front of you can assist with planning your time and can help you make decisions more quickly. For example, if you have eight things to do at work this week and two of them are similar, you might be able to get them done at the same time or back-to-back. Having the list will also remind you of high priority items, especially of those important early morning meetings.

People maintain To-Do lists in a variety of ways. You can simply keep them on yellow post-it stickies and carry them around with you. Other people like to keep white boards in their office so that their list can be viewed and shared with others. This is a good idea for team goals. With modern technology, many people are maintaining electronic To-Do lists now on the computer or blackberry. This has an added benefit of sending you notices when you have a meeting or some other reminder set up. For example, if you must submit a timesheet or any other report every other Friday, make a re-occurring appointment in your online calendar at 8:00 a.m. and you will get a reminder as soon as you log in every other Friday. Another great perk of storing this list electronically includes being able to add, change, or remove tasks effortlessly. When you store them on paper, you have to constantly cross things off and re-write the list. Additionally, when your To-Do list is stored electronically, you can simply cut and paste each item onto your status report when it is completed.

Status Reports

A status report is just as important as a To-Do list because it records your accomplishments. This can be used by you as a record of your achievements and you can present the list to your boss on a weekly basis. You can also maintain the highlights and use it during your annual performance evaluation and even if you want to negotiate for a salary increase or promotion. A status report should be a little more organized than a To-Do list so that information is clearly conveyed. You can group the information by what was accomplished each day or you can group it by work category. For example, if you are a hairdresser or barber, you might make a weekly list of how many haircuts you did, how many phone calls you took, and how many appointments you scheduled. When you finish creating a status report and look back at what you have done, you will have a great feeling of accomplishment. This can be an invaluable tool to ensure that a lot of work gets done and that priorities are attended.

Once you have created a couple of weekly or monthly status reports, review them carefully to see how you have spent your time. This can tell you a lot about the kind of employee you are. If you group the status report by each day, then you may notice certain days or times when you are more productive than others. Perhaps you have a lot of energy on Mondays but it slowly diminishes throughout the week. If this is the case, then you can try to schedule important tasks to be accomplished on Mondays so that you are working optimally. Alternatively, if you group your status reports by work category, like the hairdresser/barber mentioned earlier, then you can see how much time you spend on each major task. This is important because you can analyze it to see if you are focusing on the correct tasks.

Maintaining a status report is a great way to make sure you are staying on track for your career goals and performing the work you were hired to do. In order to ensure that this is happening, you should group your status report by the top three to five major categories of work that you are supposed to be performing. Then create a "miscellaneous" category for any other tasks that you perform and maintain the list accordingly. If you are wasting too much time on tasks you are not supposed to do, then show the reports to your boss and ask them for help with correcting the situation. For example, if you were hired to be a travel agent but you spend a lot of time making coffee and photocopying reports for the owner, then perhaps you have lost focus. Fortunately, you can show the status reports to your boss and provide documented proof that your time is not allocated appropriately. Then you can work together or at least negotiate for improvements to get back on track. These kinds of tools are all meant to help you perform your job better and to be more focused and successful.

Wasted Time

As part of being organized, we all must make sure not to waste time. After all, our time is precious and we want to use it optimally. The faster and more efficiently we can get our work done, the more time we will have for fun and leisure activities. So, how much time do you spend on unproductive tasks each day? Maybe you don't even realize when it is happening. Or maybe you do realize it, but you don't know how to stop it from happening. In order to be more organized and focused on your work, pay attention to the things that cause you to waste time. ***Choose at least three time wasters below and make concrete plans to reduce it from happening in the future:***

<u>Time Waster</u>	<u>What I will do to combat it</u>
Searching for misplaced items	
Co-workers who drop by to chat	
Personal phone calls	

Unscheduled meetings	
Having inaccurate information	
Inability to say "no"	
Indecision	
Inadequate instructions	
Waiting for approval or autho-rization from someone else	
Emergency items that come up	
Doing another person's job	

Set Boundaries And Recharge

In order to maintain organization, it is also important to set boundaries on what we will and will not do and to take time to recharge as needed. We are human and can't be perfect. We also can't be "on" and operating at 100% all of the time. Setting boundaries is important because it allows you to focus on your priorities. For example, if you need to focus on a major project and you do not want any distractions, set a specific time in your schedule and inform your co-workers that you can not be disturbed. In some cases, you can forward your calls to voice mail or even work out of a conference room where there are less distractions. If you work in a cube, ask your company about implementing a red flag system. Little red flags can be purchased relatively cheaply and employees can post them on top of their cubicles when they can not be disturbed. This is great for people who do not have doors to close. Please just make sure not to abuse the policy and keep the flag up all the time. Setting boundaries also includes your personal time. You might want to set up some rules for yourself like leaving work by 7:00 p.m. each night or turning off the blackberry on Saturdays so that you have more focused time for a personal life.

It is also important to continually assess your workload to see if it can be done more efficiently or delegated to someone else. Don't be afraid to say "no" if the work is not appropriate or it will distract you from your core duties. If you are maintaining a status report then your boss already knows how busy you are. If people try to give you additional tasks that are outside your job description, weigh your options carefully and learn to say no when appropriate. Also learn to delegate tasks as needed. There may be other people in your department or company who would enjoy certain tasks that you currently perform and it may help them to advance their career. Make sure they are willing and able to do the work and make sure to train them thoroughly. This will give you time to focus on more important tasks.

As you are keeping a reality check on your workload, keep your ego in check too. You are not a superhero and should not be expected to be all things to all people. Always take some time to focus on yourself and your own needs. Also, make sure to track your accomplishments and reward yourself. That is a common theme you will see throughout this book. Set up small rewards for yourself like a celebratory drink with friends or even just doing a happy dance with your co-workers. If you celebrate your accomplishments, you will automatically be driven for more and more success. Take time each day to think and reflect, even if it is just five minutes during your lunch hour or during your commute. Try to plan for time off each month, even if it is just a long weekend. Also make sure to schedule honest to goodness vacation time and try to do it in advance so that your boss is aware and you have time to plan and look forward to it. You can even post pictures of upcoming vacations in your work space to generate even more excitement. Keeping your life well-rounded like this will enhance every aspect of it.

Conclusion

Getting organized is the first major step toward becoming a happier and more successful employee. No matter what level of organizational skills you have now, you can make improvements to be even better. This is an important topic because being disorganized can make you look like a bad employee and can stifle your future career potential. On the other hand, maintaining a sense of organization at work can enhance your reputation, allow you to save time, reduce your stress level, and it allows others to work with you more easily. The benefits are tremendous because you are more in control of your schedule and ultimately of the path your career will take.

The important aspects of being organized at work only begin with your physical work space. Keeping a clean and orderly environment is just the baseline toward being successful. It is also important to fully understand your work assignments and make sure you are performing the appropriate tasks. An operator's manual is key to ensuring that tasks are performed accurately and maintaining To-Do lists and status reports ensure that you are focused on the right tasks. Since we all have time wasters in our environment, we all must be diligent to reduce or stop these kinds of distractions. Once these tasks are all in place, set boundaries, celebrate accomplishments, and take time to recharge as needed. Having organizational skills is the same as any other kind of talent, like tennis or playing the flute, you will get better at it over time. It just takes practice. Once you get more organized, you will feel a better sense of well being, and you will be able to focus on the next step, which is about knowing your purpose and setting goals for the future.

Ch. 3 – Approach Your Job With Purpose And Set Goals

It is not enough to be busy; so are the ants. The question is: what are we busy about? --Henry David Thoreau

Everyone has purpose in life. Something motivates you to get out of bed each morning and go to work. What specifically motivates you? Is it because you look forward to seeing your co-workers, you are anxious to get started on a project, you are eager to share information with your boss, or is it that you just don't want to get fired? If it is the last one, then your motivation is money and security.

What tasks do you enjoy doing most? What are you most complimented on? What makes you feel good? These are important things to know about yourself in order to learn to love your job. Some people like to take life as it comes but this just shows a lack of purpose. Your purpose comes from what you most value. In order to be successful with anything, it all starts with purpose. Then to expand on the purpose, you must set goals to achieve the next level of success. As you achieve your goals or the smaller tasks associated with them called milestones, you should recognize your hard work and reward yourself.

It is not *just* about making a list of goals and setting out to achieve them, it is about knowing what you want out of your career and making calculated decisions in order to make your dreams a reality. The goals must compliment each other so that all of your dreams can be realized. It takes active participation on your part to create a plan and constant follow-up to make sure you stay on track, but the possible rewards are limitless. On the other hand, if you feel like every day is the same thing, you don't get excited, and nothing new ever happens, then you are not living life with purpose and you are probably not working toward any specific career goals. This chapter will help you to make improvements in these areas.

Approach Your Job With Purpose

When you approach your job with purpose, you fully understand your role and how it fits into the global needs of the company. You also have future career goals that you are working toward. Having purpose means being mindful about what you are doing and acknowledging both your own efforts and those of others. It is about noticing the details and caring about what is happening. The quintessential example of a lack of purpose is from the movie, *Joe Versus the Volcano* where people walked to work with a glazed look in their eyes and didn't seem to care or even notice about anything going on around them. When you lead life with purpose, it is easier to make decisions because you already understand what you want. To approach your job with purpose is to carry out the tasks you want to do. If you are not doing your job purposefully then you are just letting circumstances carry you through. Finding your purpose can make you feel better, perform better, and recognize your own success. It can also make you feel more confidence and have less anxiety, anger, stress, fear, and worry.

Employees who approach their job with purpose clearly understand their current job description and have goals set for future career advancement. With this kind of structure in place, it is easier to make decisions based on accomplishing these goals and it is more rewarding to track your progress. When you know your purpose, you will have a desire to continually grow and expand. For example, if a bookkeeper dreams of one day becoming a certified public accountant, they will take courses, attend conferences, subscribe to journal articles, and continually try to upgrade their knowledge and skill set to achieve that goal. People who are not driven to learn more about their job and how they can add value to their company are usually stuck in a rut and do not have high hopes for their future career or their financial growth. To these people, the future looks the same as the past. In order to combat this and have dreams for a better future, it is important to have a mission and a direction in your work life.

Understand Your Purpose

There are two primary documents that will help you to understand your purpose at your company. Those documents are your job description and your performance evaluations. If you do not have a written job description, then create one right now. If you have one but have not reviewed it in a while, take it out and review plus update it now. If you do not have access to it, ask your boss or the human resource department. If they want to know why you are asking for it, tell them about this great book you are reading.

This process is important because your job should be constantly evolving as you grow and change. As a new employee, it may take a while to learn new tasks and understand the work flow. However, over time, you should master each task and be able to complete projects faster. That way you can take on more work and try to progress to higher levels in the company. Additionally, technology is always advancing and laws are always changing so there is constant opportunity to modernize systems and processes. You should continually look for better ways to do your job and update your job description accordingly. Then your hard work should be reflected on your performance evaluations.

A good place to start is with a careful analysis of your job description. Your job description should be clearly written and reviewed or updated at least every six months. Your job description should begin with a brief summary of the purpose of your job. For example, an administrative assistant might write:

> **Purpose**: I assist the V.P of Product Development by
> answering phones, scheduling appointments, creating
> monthly product reports, and maintaining the product files. I
> also serve as back-up to the main receptionist as needed.

It may seem like a tough task, but it is important to summarize your major duties into one cohesive statement before you can further breakdown your job into its more basic components. ***List the purpose of your current position in two to three sentences below:***

_____

_____

_____

_____

If you do not have a written job description, then you can use this as a starting point. Then, after you have written your purpose, make a list of each task you perform and the approximate amount of time spent on each task. Make sure to be specific and include any timelines. For example, one task might be: "create ABC report every Thursday and submit it to Jane Smith, John Nolan, and Terry Bolls." If you are feeling very bold you can separate the essential functions of the job from the non-essential functions of the job. Make sure to include every task you perform along with the timing that it is due. Having a written job description is important to clarify your role and expectations.

After your job description is clearly written, review your latest performance evaluation. Are you achieving the goals you set out to accomplish? Were the goals clear and measurable? If not, how can you create more realistic goals in the future so that you can be rewarded? Employees typically only look at their performance evaluations when they are initially handed to them. However, it is very important to read them periodically, even once a month. The goals section of the performance evaluation is a major priority but it is also important to re-read all of the feedback you received. First start by looking at your strengths and reflect on all the positive things you do. Are there ways you can enhance these qualities even more? Then look at areas that need improvement. It is not always easy to receive constructive criticism, but these are usually "growth opportunities" that can only make us better and stronger employees.

Let's look at your assets a little more closely. Do you have an advanced degree in your field? Are you a superstar at creating PowerPoint presentations? ***List three tasks that you perform really well or other qualities that you bring to the table:***

1.

2.

3.

Now list one thing about yourself that you would like to improve. Don't be shy, no one is perfect and we can always make changes for the better:

1.

This process is almost like giving yourself a mini self evaluation. So, how do you think you are doing? Are you making a significant impact on your organization? Is it a better company because you work there? How do you go above and beyond your job description? Are you getting better at your job every year? It is important to know yourself including the qualities you bring to the table and the areas that you need to improve. When you have a clear job description and you know your assets, then you will be well on your way to planning a bright future career. Start thinking about what you want to accomplish and what your five, ten, and twenty-year work goals should look like. Once you have a long term plan, you can set up shorter term goals or milestones to achieve along the way toward realizing all of your dreams.

Work Goals

It is important to have goals in life in order to realize your purpose and direction. We all have hopes and dreams. However, the people who make clear written goals with action items for achieving them, are much more likely to achieve their goals and are happier and more successful people as a result. If you have not created a clear list of career goals within the last six months, then this section is for you. Having goals allows you to track how far you have come in the past and where you are going in the future. This helps you to have focus and direction but also allows you to celebrate successes.

So, are you headed where you want to go? Or are you just reacting, moment by moment, to whatever is happening to you right now? Do you feel that you are in control of your destiny? Understanding your purpose and setting out to achieve work goals can change your whole career. It puts you in the driver's seat. For example, where do you want your career to be in five and ten years from now? Will you be at the same company and in the same position? Maybe you would like to be at the same company but in a higher position? Or maybe you would like to be in a different department performing completely different tasks? These may be tough questions to answer right now, but you need to think about these things so that you can plan for your future. If you don't, who will?

No matter what your career or profession is, you should always have a dream to go higher and achieve more. Perhaps you had goals and dreams a long time ago but they have been forgotten. If so, now is the time to bring them back to life. Perhaps there are qualities that you admire in others that you would like to foster within yourself. Or maybe you simply want the financial security of attaining a higher level position. *It really is possible.* You just need to start building a plan. The next few sections will help you to develop a clear set of written career goals. Having goals and dreams and then setting out to pursue them is one of the most rewarding and enjoyable things we can do in life. If you have lost focus on your goals, it is time to get back on track.

Fundamentals Of Goal Setting

Creating career goals can be a fun process because you can be creative and let your imagination run wild. Start with brainstorming a list of every detail that you want to achieve in your career. Do you want to manage and lead a group of people? Would you like to build something and work with your hands? Maybe you would like to be doing something more artistic and creative? Try to be as specific as possible so that you can really imagine yourself achieving the goal. Write out each detail and then choose the top priorities from your list. It is best to pick three to five complimentary goals and then set out to achieve them in order. For example, you might want to obtain your masters degree in literature, then write a book about great American poets, and then obtain a part-time teaching job at your local college.

Brainstorming is the fun part but once you select concrete goals that you really want to set out to achieve, make sure they are realistic and attainable. Here are some guidelines to get you started:

1. The goal must be something that you truly want for yourself and not something that someone else wants, like your parents or your spouse, or even a pipe dream you had as a kid. Did you want to be a movie star because you truly enjoy acting or just for the money and fame?

2. Next, make sure your goals are realistic. If you have a goal to win a million dollars in the lottery, that may not actually be attainable. A goal is something that you have control over.

3. Break each goal down into smaller milestones that will be achieved in order to reach the goal. For example, if you plan to get your masters degree within two years then you might want to map out how many classes you will need to take each semester.

4. Track your progress and stay positive. Keep your goals posted in a place where you can see them on a regular basis. Every time you make a decision, ask if it coincides with your planned goals.

5. Most importantly, celebrate successes. Each time you achieve a milestone, savor the moment and give yourself a pat on the back.

Create A Personalized Goal Plan

In this section, you will be asked to create a list of short term and long term career goals that you would like to achieve. Follow the guidelines above and create goals that are specific, realistic, and attainable. It is important to understand exactly what you want so that you can plan for it to happen and so that you can celebrate your success once it does happen.

You should be able to clearly define what you want and be able to map out each step to get there. You should also determine if you have all the tools and resources necessary to make it happen. Be aware of obstacles you may encounter and set plans in motion beforehand so that you can be more proactive than reactive. After the goals are set, break each one down into the milestones that will be needed to get there. Set dates for completion and plans for ways you will reward yourself when they are achieved.

Let's start. Create three short term goals and three long term goals for your career. Short term goals can be achieved within the next 6-12 months. Long term goals can be achieved within the next 1-5 years. Examples of short term work goals may be to finish a particular project at work, develop a skill set like becoming more organized, or maybe improving a current process that is not working well. Examples of long term goals may be to get a certain raise next year, to take on additional responsibility, or to manage more people.

A. List your specific goals here:

Short term goals (6-12 months)

1.

2.

3.

Long term goals (1-5 years)

1.

2.

3.

Now take one of the goals you mentioned above and let's really develop it. If your goal is to become more organized, then you can create smaller milestones to make that happen. For example, you might want to buy a book about organizational skills, attend a seminar, and make a commitment to clean certain sections of your work space every week for the next two months. Milestones are great because they are "small wins" that can give you a feeling of accomplishment. They help you to see your progress and allow you to take a break and smell the roses. This will motivate you to keep going onward and upward.

B. Develop one of your goals:

Details of the goal:

Start date:

Anticipated completion date:

List each milestone, in chronological order, that will be needed to achieve this goal:

Milestone	Anticipated Completion date
1.	
2.	
3.	

4.	
5.	

What tools or resources will you need to achieve this goal?

Who will help you to achieve this?

Cost? (if any)

Benefits:

Rewards

The best part about achieving goals and even the smaller milestones, are the associated rewards. There is certainly intrinsic value in achieving any goal that is set, but you can also reinforce it with other things that make you feel good. Are you one of those people who have a candy jar at your desk? Do you munch on treats throughout the day? Try using them as a reward instead and only partake when you have something to celebrate, even if it is a very small win.

Let's continue the exercise from the previous section. You started to clearly develop a particular goal and the milestones associated with it. Now imagine that you have surpassed every milestone and have achieved the goal. How will you celebrate? When the goal is achieved, you can add the following questions to the Goal Plan so that every-thing is together. This helps keep everything organized and reinforces the great feeling of success.

C. Imagine you have achieved the goal that you developed. Then answer the following questions:

What did you achieve?

How does it feel?

What was the impact of this on others?

How do you plan to enjoy this success?

What area do you want to focus on next?

Make sure you plan ahead so that you have everything you need, including the time, ability, and resources to accomplish each milestone. Talk with people who have achieved similar goals to get their advice. You don't always need to re-invent the wheel. Share ideas and network. Also use various people for support. Then be there when they need a helping hand in return. We are all in this together.

Here are some examples of how you can reward yourself:
(Please note that some of these examples are repeated in other section of this book)

- ✓ Take a walk around the building or in a natural setting
- ✓ Eat a tasty treat or go all out and have a hot fudge sundae
- ✓ Plan to have lunch with a friend or go shopping
- ✓ Play a round of golf or any other sport you enjoy
- ✓ Schedule a massage
- ✓ Buy a new suit

✓ Have a little parade around the office to celebrate a big win

✓ Plan a weekend away or other time off with family/friends

✓ Start planning now and have $25 per paycheck diverted to a savings account and use that as fun money to reward yourself after achieving major milestones

You should feel good about rewarding yourself. Rewards are a nice way to give yourself a pat on the back for a job well done. Celebrating milestones is the key to meeting your goals. If everyone waited until the end of a project to celebrate, a lot of goals would be dropped. People just would not make it past many obstacles. Rewards should be fun and creative. If you run out of ideas, ask your boss, friends, family, or co-workers for ideas. They know you well and may have some great suggestions. You can even play a game with it and write each little reward on a slip of paper and put them into a jar and pull them out when you achieve a milestone. The sky is the limit and you are in control of your destiny.

Staying On Track

Now you have your current purpose clear and future goals set. Next let's focus on keeping the momentum. What does it take for you to be happy and fulfilled in your job? Do you like to have recognition from your boss and/or co-workers? Or do you prefer to have new and creative challenges? Or do you like things to remain steady and consistent? Find out what you need and set the tone accordingly. Once you clearly understand your goals and what sort of environment you need to achieve them, communicate it to others around you. Then they can support you in the process.

Share your goals with your boss, your co-workers, and also your family and friends. Don't tell people who are negative or try to discourage you. Avoid those people. Allow for flexibility so if your exact original plan does not work out, you don't have to stop, instead you just re-adjust. Anyone can get sidetracked or discouraged from time to time. Just get back on track and remember to focus on the goals, stay positive, and reward yourself for completing milestones. Envision what it will be like to achieve the goal and you will get there in no time.

If you continue to feel discouraged, it might be appropriate to take a step back and assess whether the goals are realistic and attainable in the time frame that you set for yourself. Have you clearly identified all of the obstacles or have new ones popped up that you need to analyze and combat? Are you using all of your resources properly? Could anyone else help you? Or are you just procrastinating and need a boost? A great way to get a boost is to imagine that you have achieved the goal already. For example, if one of your milestones is to get an advanced degree in a certain subject, then print a picture of what the diploma will look like and hang it over your computer. If you want a promotion, write your new title on a piece of paper and use that as motivation. Have fun with this and be creative.

Conclusion

How do you know that you are approaching your job with purpose? Measure the results. Are you doing everything the same way you did a year ago? If yes, make improvements. Research a certain aspect of your job and give a presentation to your boss or co-workers. Ask to take a seminar on time management or communication skills. You can also simply buy a book about your career goals. You can even do research on the internet for free and learn about the latest trends and techniques that people are using in your industry. Employees who approach their job with purpose are passionate about their jobs and eager to learn more and contribute to the company's success.

Once you understand your overall purpose, it is important to create or update your job description and review your most recent performance evaluations. Your job description should list your purpose and summarize the major tasks that you perform. When reviewing your performance evaluation, make sure you are on track to achieve the goals. Then make plans to create even more goals for your next evaluation. If your company does not administer performance evaluations, you can conduct a self assessment at any time. This can help you to realize your strengths and areas that need improvement. Knowing yourself is important if you want to set future goals.

The next step is to create those goals and anticipate each milestone that will need to be achieved. Each goal will be more easily attainable if it clearly written with such detail that you can imagine yourself in the moment that it is achieved. Rewarding yourself along the way is an important step because it keeps you on track and motivated toward further success. The rewards should be fun and unique to your personality. If you still get sidetracked from your goals, look for support from your boss or co-workers and allow flexibility so that you can make adjustments if needed. When you finally achieve each goal, take a step back and enjoy the sweet smell of success. Having carefully constructed work goals puts you in control of your future career path and can be very rewarding and give you positive energy. The next chapter takes this a step further and discusses how to promote a positive attitude in all areas of your job.

Ch. 4 – Choose To Have A Positive Attitude

Whether you think you can or think you can't - you are right.
--Henry Ford

Do you really want to know the secret of being happy in life? The secret is… to be happy. You just make a conscious choice to be happy with what you have and to cope proactively with any problems or obstacles you face, and that is it. It is all about you because you have the power to turn your life around. You can choose to be happy or unhappy, it is up to you. It takes just as much effort to be negative and unhappy as it does to be positive and happy. So, why not focus on the good stuff? Let's look at a couple of scenarios.

> **Scenario # 1** – You wake up to the buzzing alarm clock and dread the idea of getting up so you hit the snooze button several times and try to get a few more minutes of sleep. You eventually stumble out of bed, skip breakfast to save time, and find clothes to wear. Of course there is always traffic and everyone else is a bad driver so you grip the steering wheel hard and curse under your breath at the other drivers while you bob and weave through traffic. As this is going on, you have these negative scripts running through your head like, "I am going to be late, I am going to be late" or "I hate my lousy job." You get to the office a few minutes late and dodge your boss, walking the long way around, so that they (hopefully) won't notice. You get coffee to try and wake up and stare bewilderingly at your overwhelming workload wondering where to start first.

Or

> **Scenario # 2** – You wake up a few minutes before your alarm goes off because you are eager to start the day. Your clothes are ready and your To-Do list is planned so you know where you need to be and when. On the way to work, you become

engrossed in a new CD you bought about being a positive thinker. You arrive a little early and have time to chat with a co-worker and compliment him on his new suit. It makes you feel good to make others smile. You greet your boss with a confident "hello" and let her know your report will be ready on time. Then you tackle your work with conviction and purpose, knowing that your future will just keep getting brighter.

So, which way do you live your life? Are you in control of the situation or just taking things as they come? You have the ability to live each day being happy and productive or negative and complacent. Which way are you choosing to live? You are the person who controls your feelings and reactions. Not anyone else. It is up to you whether you maintain control of that or if you allow others to control your emotions, how you feel, and ultimately what decisions you make. Don't let any other person take that power away from you. When you come across an aggressive driver who cuts you off in traffic, interact with a co-worker who snaps at you because they are having a bad day, or get yelled at by your boss because they are under a lot of pressure, don't take it personally and allow it to affect the way you feel. Look at each situation objectively and learn to accept that there will be problems in life, but you can deal with them effectively and then move onward and upward. This chapter will help you to learn these techniques.

Attitude Assessment

On a scale of 1-10, with 10 being the best, rate yourself on the following:

I feel that my overall attitude is:

1   2   3   4   5   6   7   8   9   10

If I were to guess how my boss would rate me, it would be:

1   2   3   4   5   6   7   8   9   10

If I were to guess how my co-workers would rate me, it would be:

1   2   3   4   5   6   7   8   9   10

The level of patience I show to others is:

1   2   3   4   5   6   7   8   9   10

When faced with a problem or opposition from someone, I am able to forget it and move on quickly:

1   2   3   4   5   6   7   8   9   10

When changes occur, I am able to acclimate to the new way quickly:

1   2   3   4   5   6   7   8   9   10

I feel that my knowledge, skills, and abilities are being used properly:

1   2   3   4   5   6   7   8   9   10

I feel that I get the recognition I deserve for my contributions:

1   2   3   4   5   6   7   8   9   10

I am able to incorporate humor into each workday:

1   2   3   4   5   6   7   8   9   10

I would recommend others to work for this company:

1   2   3   4   5   6   7   8   9   10

Total Score: _____

Benefits Of A Positive Attitude

Having a positive attitude means that you are generally optimistic and are hopeful about the future. It does not mean that you have to be happy all the time or phony in the way you treat people. However, it does involve being polite, being open to new ideas and changes, and being able to cope and work through problems. This means that when something bad happens, you accept it as a fact of life and move on. Don't dwell on negative things or anticipate unhappy future events. It is much more rewarding to imagine a bright future and expect good things to happen to you. Take a moment now and think of three good things that happened to you in the last week. Was someone exceptionally polite? Did you receive a compliment? Maybe you finished a project within schedule? How often do you spend time reflecting on the positive aspects of life?

When you have a positive attitude, you expect and plan for good things to happen. Then good things happen as a result. You tend to see opportunities more clearly and look for solutions rather than dwelling on the problems and feeling helpless. This can help you to achieve your goals more easily and allow you to enjoy the journey along the way. This happens because you tend to work harder and are less likely to give up on things. When you think positive, you have more energy, more people want to help and support you, and your career will ultimately be more successful. Having a positive attitude is also contagious and can boost the spirit of others and spread the good vibrations. Additionally, people with a positive attitude tend to lead happier lives, are more successful, and have lower stress levels and blood pressure.

Alternatively, being angry, having a negative attitude, and feeling stressed out can cause a variety of health problems from high blood pressure, heart disease, depression, and even the common cold. Being negative and unhappy also takes a lot of energy and can leave you feeling empty and tired. Negativity can also spread, just like positive energy can. When you are feeling down and depressed, it tends to bring down all of the people around you, who might have otherwise been happy. This not only affects the way your boss and co-workers feel about you but it can trickle into your personal life and affect your marriage or even your ability to be a good parent too. Think about this: are you a good role model for your children and would you be happy for them if they grew up to be the same way? Would you want to be married to you? Would you want to be your boss? Think about your attitude on a daily basis and always try to make it better.

How To Spend Your Day

Many people will be shocked to learn that it is not enough to show up to work every day and fulfill the obligations of the job. You can not just complete your assigned tasks and go home. If only it were that easy! We also have to work with people, impress our boss, support our co-workers, and typically deal with customers. We do not work in a bubble and there will always be bumps and turns in the road. We must learn to be flexible about change, cope with problems, and continually seek to make improvements in our quality of work. When employees take pride in their work it shows. These are the people that look at the company as a whole and want the entire team to be successful and not just themselves. These are the people who are looking positively into the future and do not dwell on the past. These are all the things we must do as employees. And yes, it is possible for each end every one of us to make the choice to live this way.

Having a positive attitude starts the moment you wake up each morning. Make sure to sleep well, eat healthy, and most importantly to wake up on time. This sets the tone for the day and allows you to get to work on time and be prepared. When you get to work, have a fresh mindset every day. Greet everyone warmly with a smile and friendly demeanor. Never be a complainer. No one likes to be around that type of person. If you are having personal problems, do not vent or complain to co-workers. They are not there to be your therapist. Separate your personal life from your professional life. If you are having a work related problem then address it rather than letting it fester. If you have a problem that you can not solve, ask for help from your boss or co-workers. Then help them in return when they need it. If you focus more on solving problems rather than complaining about them, people will notice.

Thinking positive means that you appreciate the good things that are happening and do not dwell on the negative. Remember this and give sincere appreciation to others when they do a good job, even if their tasks do not directly relate to you. The company is a giant team and if others are successful then you will be successful too. However if you do make mistakes, as we all do because we are human, be honest and own up to it. Covering mistakes will only get you into trouble in the long run and will cause you added stress. Always set out to make your boss and co-workers look good. Come to work every day ready to work and eager to make a contribution. Treat your job as if you owned the company and you will make smarter decisions about spending money and allocating resources. This will make you stand out from the crowd and impress the management team.

Here are some quick tips for maintaining a positive attitude at work:

- ✓ Do your job better than you have to

- ✓ Be flexible to change

- ✓ Don't take it personally if someone doesn't treat you right

✓ Be extra nice to new employees and go out of your way to make them feel welcome

✓ Recognize both the good qualities and the achievements of others and genuinely compliment at least one person a day

✓ Show appreciation when someone helps you even if it is small act

✓ Don't complain for complaining sake; if there is a problem, look to be a problem-solver and resolve the issue before it affects anyone else

✓ Look for the silver lining in any obstacles you come across

✓ Make a list of ways you will cope with problems if they happen

✓ Be open to constructive criticism because it is one of the few ways you can grow and become better

✓ Don't be afraid to say you are sorry if you are wrong, it does not make you look weak, it make you look strong and secure (not to mention honest)

✓ Plan for happiness and expect your future to be bright

Motivation

Having a positive attitude does not just happen automatically. Although it gets easier over time with practice, it does take work. The key here is in being motivated to make active changes. We can be motivated for many different reasons. Sometimes the reasons are "intrinsic" or internal within ourselves, such as doing a job for the feeling of pride or accomplishment it brings. Other times the reasons are "extrinsic" or externally outside of ourselves, like receiving money or praise from others. Each person is unique in what motivates them. We all have basic human needs and like to eat and have a roof over our head, but after those basic needs are met, we tend to want our higher level needs to be fulfilled like self-esteem, respect by others, and achievement. Although we all share these basic needs, we all strive for them in different ways. It is important as individuals to know what unique factors will motivate us the most toward being successful.

Your *intrinsic* motivation is important because it has to do with your work ethic and the way you feel about your job. It involves your natural propensity to be curious about your environment and wanting to accomplish a task because it is interesting, challenging, or enjoyable. For example, a marketing manager might enjoy creating an advertising campaign and they might spend a lot of overtime making it perfect because they enjoy the process. However that same person might have their eyes gloss over at the idea of creating a budget spreadsheet and they might procrastinate past the deadline. The tasks and situations that might intrinsically motivate you are probably very different from your co-workers. Either way, employers seek to find employees who are intrinsically motivated toward their job because they are more proactive and tend to have a better attitude. These people typically have more control over their feelings and emotions and have a steadier work output because they are more introverted and their energy comes from within, not by whatever circumstances happen to be going on around them.

Your *extrinsic* motivation is more tangible and has to do with the rewards and punishment in your environment that move you toward completing tasks. It is more about engaging in an activity as a means to an end, rather than genuinely enjoying the process. This kind of motivation is more controlled by others with rewards like raises or recognition along with punishments like reprimands or simply the fear of being fired. For example, a dentist might enjoy working with clients but hate completing insurance paperwork, but they do it anyway because they have to in order to get paid. Extrinsic motivators can be a strong force in controlling how we behave at work. However, extrinsic motivation is not always sustainable in a consistent manner over time. If you receive a raise after completing a project, you will probably feel good about it for a few weeks, but it doesn't last forever. You will want another raise eventually and particularly so after you complete another similar project. The problem with external motivators is that they must be consistently changed or increased over time in order to continue having the same effect and keep people motivated.

The important thing about motivation is in understanding what unique factors motivate you. To begin with, everyone should have intrinsic motivation to do their job well. If you do not have intrinsic motivation then you should take a serious look at your career and commit to make changes to your situation. That might mean bringing a new energy and enthusiasm to your current job or changing careers into something that will truly inspire you. Additionally, you should know what kind of extrinsic motivators will affect you the most. Do you want more money or would you prefer to have more vacation time? Do you get jazzed up over the idea of being assigned a new and creative project or do you prefer your current tasks? If you know what motivates you then you can use it to be even more successful. Make sure to always be aware of the internal and external motivators in your environment. Everyone should have a good balance between intrinsic and extrinsic motivation but your best bet is not to look for happiness and fulfillment externally, true happiness comes from within.

Self Scripts

Everyone carries on conversations in their mind and has scripts running through their head. Often as soon as we wake up in the morning, we run through a mental To-Do list of things we need to accomplish and we carry on this self talk throughout the day. Sometimes these scripts are positive but often they are negative. For example, if you are running late to work, you might have the same negative script running over and over through your head, "I am going to be late, I am going to be late." Or maybe just before an important meeting or presentation you are thinking, "they are going to hate it." This kind of self talk has a direct affect on your emotions and behaviors. Having these kinds of scripts can prevent you from being motivated and is a major contributor to a negative attitude. It also distracts you from getting your job done well and ultimately leads to poor performance. It can be a self fulfilling prophecy that whatever you are thinking will happen.

When your internal scripts are positive, you expect and plan subconsciously for positive things to happen. You see opportunities more clearly and recognize good investments. The opposite happens when you have negative scripts running through your mind. In fact, when that happens, it shows that you are not even trying to be successful. You are letting your external environment completely control you. It also causes more stress and can promote depression when having self destructive thoughts constantly running through your mind. It is so frustrating to see people living this way. Often it is a result of how you were raised because sometimes your self scripts are inherited. Ask yourself this, would I want to talk to my children the way I am talking to myself? If the answer is "no" then you need to make some serious changes. It can be very difficult to change this because it is a common habit that has typically been happening for years. However if you use some behavior modification techniques then you can start feeling better almost instantly.

A good way to start this transformation is to keep track of your scripts throughout the day and count which ones are positive versus negative. You can keep a notepad or a little stickie note at your desk and keep score of every positive and negative thought that you have throughout the work day. If you perform a task well and think to yourself, "good job" then give yourself a check in the positive category. If you make a mistake and think to yourself, "I am such an idiot" then give yourself a check in the negative category. If you have more negative thoughts throughout the day, then you should make an effort to change them into positive ones. For each negative thought, first evaluate it further to see if the thought is even realistic. This involves separating the facts from the emotion. Then analyze whether it is benefitting you in any way to have these kinds of thoughts or if they are just bringing yourself and others down. The goal is to challenge your negative thinking and to turn it around into more productive and positive planning.

You can flip the negative into the positive by simply forming an opposite statement. Instead of, "my boss is going to hate this" turn it into "my boss is going to love this." You can also be creative in your imagination and think about how much your boss will love it, what he or she will say, and the rewards you will receive as a result. If you want your new script to be more personalized, you can add your preferences. For example, instead of, "Jenny is probably coming over here to complain about something" try "I bet Jenny is coming over here to compliment me on my speech yesterday and she is going to pay me back the $10 she owes me." It takes work to change your internal scripts but if you practice on a daily basis, then more positive and realistic thinking will become automatic and second nature.

Write 3-4 negative scripts that you have said to yourself in the last few days and create new more positive scripts that you will replace them with in the future:

Current negative script...	New positive script...
1.	
2.	
3.	
4.	

Dealing With Negativity At Work

Negative people often have low self esteem, poor morale, and are not as mature as others. People who feel good about themselves tend to see new situations as challenges and are eager to learn new things. However, people who see themselves as failures tend to see new situations as threats and feel they will make mistakes and be caused stress.

They get defensive about change or any new ideas because they always look toward the future with anxiety and stress. When you encounter negativity in others, you can either provoke it further by adding your own negative thoughts until it snowballs, or you can allow it to diminish by refusing to counter it with your own negativity. In fact, there are things you can do to cope with and reduce the negativity that goes on around you at work. There are common mistakes that people make with the way they view situations and these mistakes often cause a lot of negativity. If you become more aware of these kinds of issues, you can try to avoid it in your own life.

Here are some common pitfalls that contribute to negativity at work:

Exaggeration
When people make something bigger than it really is.

Personalization
When people personalize situations and assume it is all about them.

Overgeneralization
Taking an isolated incident and blowing it out of proportion.

Jumping to conclusions
Making a conclusion before gathering all the facts.

Displacement
When our feelings toward one person, who is typically more powerful, are directed at someone else, who is typically less powerful.

The important thing is to be aware of these obstacles so that you don't fall into these traps. Separate the facts from the emotion and look at each situation objectively. When others around you are being negative, try to have patience and if at all possible, turn their negativity into positivity. For example, remember that chronically negative people are negative with everyone, it's not about you. So if a negative person is having a bad day and snaps at you, don't personalize it and think that they are out to get you. They are just unhappy with the world and not seeing the actual situation clearly. Maybe they just need time and space to process a recent event or come to a solution on their own. Otherwise, you can immediately try to defuse the anger by speaking in a calm tone and listening to everything they have to say so that you have all the facts. For example, if someone yells at you and you get upset and yell back, then it just inflames the situation. It is better if you talk slowly and calmly because that tends to calm them down.

Being in control like this will give you an inner sense of calmness and make you feel in control of the situation. However, it does not mean that you are a doormat that should take abuse or that you are the company therapist and should listen to an employee's personal problems. If it is a legitimate work issue then let the angry person vent their feelings while you focus on what they are trying to say. When they are done, summarize what you heard and try to show empathy for their situation. This ensures that you understand the situation fully and it makes them feel like they have truly been heard. Apologize blamelessly if the situation warrants it. You don't have to say, "I am sorry that the service department ignored your request" but you can say something like, "I am sorry you are experiencing a delay, I can understand how frustrating that can be." This can help you focus on solving the problem rather than placing blame. Remember that not all problems can be solved optimally. But at least you will have shown professionalism in the face of conflict and showed sympathy and tolerance to someone who needed it.

Conclusion

Having a positive attitude does not automatically happen, you have to work at it. You must actively search for things to be happy about. You have the ability to control your own thoughts and emotions and should not allow whatever is happening in your environment to take that control away from you. When you have a positive attitude, you expect good things to happen and are hopeful for the future. Maintaining this kind of outlook can be beneficial for your energy level, productivity, long term career success, and even your overall health. It takes work though. Besides completing the tasks of your normal job, you must also interact with others and make a conscious effort to cope with and resolve problems in a proactive way.

A large factor in having a positive attitude has to do with your motivation. Different things motivate different people and it is important to know what kinds of intrinsic and extrinsic motivators you value most. Intrinsic motivators are deep within ourselves whereas extrinsic motivators are external and typically controlled by others. If you know what motivates you then you can use that to become even more successful. In order to have a positive attitude, you must also take an active approach to combating any negative thoughts or feelings you have. It starts from the moment you wake up in the morning with the kind of self scripts you allow to run through your head. Having positive scripts will give you a brighter outlook and better ensure your chances of success.

Naturally, obstacles in life will try to block your view and bring you down. When this happens, there are many typical blunders that people make. If you become aware of these common pitfalls, you can make sure they happen less frequently to you and those around you. Of course you will still have to deal with negative people from time to time. When this happens, stay calm and don't make one of those common mistakes like exaggerating the event or personalizing the situation. Always separate the facts from the emotion and speak calmly to the person who is being negative. Stay in control of your own feelings and emotions and you can become a role model for others. The next chapter presents an equally important topic, which is about the use of communication in our day-to-day interactions at work.

Ch. 5 – Be An Effective Communicator

The way we communicate with others and with ourselves ultimately determines the quality of our lives. --Tony Robbins

Have you ever received a confusing email and did not understand its purpose? Have you ever sat through a long winded speech and wished you could sneak out of the room? How about getting assigned a project and not being sure how to proceed? Has a co-worker ever been angry at you and you were not sure why? These are all problems that can occur when people do not exercise good communication skills. Communication is the process of exchanging information from one source to another. It involves someone creating a message and sending it to someone else and then that person deciphering what was received. Typically the process also includes sharing feedback between the people involved. Being a good communicator takes work and it is not a static process. It is an ongoing endeavor to ensure that the messages we send and receive are fully understood.

In today's modern work world, communications can be transmitted in a variety of different ways. Verbal communication can be shared face-to-face, over the phone, or via video or web conferencing. Written communication at work typically takes the form of email, fax, memos, or other documents such as employee manuals and procedural forms. Communication happens all day long from the minute we show up at work and greet someone at the coffee machine, to the moment we say good night at the end of the day. In between those events, we might attend a meeting, exchange email, complete some forms, give directions to a customer, and assist our boss with a presentation. Each of these events requires different forms of communication. A good communicator does not have to be exceptionally witty and have a high IQ, they just need to easily join a conversation, contribute their thoughts and ideas clearly and concisely, and be memorable. They must also be good listeners and be able to read people and situations.

When creating and sending any kind of communication, it is important to convey your message clearly and concisely so that anyone can understand what you are trying to say. The choice of words or language we use when we convey a message, along with the tone and method of delivery, influences the quality of the communication. We also must be aware of the non-verbal cues we are sending like the tone we use and our body language. All of the different aspects of the communication should match each other. For example, if we say we are happy about something but we say it through gritted teeth with a blank expression on our face, people will know we are not being honest. The total package of the communication must be complete. When receiving communication, which is just as important, the goal is to clearly understand it without any distortion. There are many steps involved in giving and receiving clear communications. This chapter reviews the entire process.

What It Means To Have Good Communication Skills

Being able to communicate with people and build relationships is one of the most important skills that we learn throughout our lives. Having good communications skills means that there will be less conflict, errors, misunderstandings, and frustration. When you communicate well, you get along better with other people from all walks of life. Your opinions and suggestions can be evaluated by others more easily. People will be able to give you what you want, simply because they will know clearly what you have asked for and why you need it. You will be more persuasive and tasks will be performed more easily. This means that you will get your point across, your ideas will be heard, and your suggestions will be implemented. You will get work done faster and easier and people will be eager to make you successful. Additionally, you will have greater confidence in your ability to understand the important information that is around you all the time.

Communication is a powerful tool because it can build, maintain, and even break down relationships. Because of this, employees should continually develop their verbal, written, and listening skills.

Information can not be effectively created, transferred, received, or exchanged without using good communication skills. The reason why we communicate at work is typically to: inform, request, persuade, or simply to build relationships. When the employees at a company communicate well together, the following benefits can be achieved:

- The company mission, vision, and values are clear to everyone

- Employees are united around common goals

- Each person understands their job description

- Performance feedback and training occur consistently

- The company policies are clearly documented and conveyed

- Productivity is high and waste is low

When communicating with others, one of the most important decisions is in how the message will be delivered. The primary choices are to communicate in either verbal or written format. Deciding which one is more ideal has to do with the message itself, the situation, and the people involved. If the message is to be delivered verbally, then the next decision is whether to do it face-to-face, over the phone, or via an electronic medium. If it is going to be a written message, the next choice is to determine whether it is via email, a mailed letter, or a variety of other options. Once you make these initial choices, the next steps are to set the tone and plan the content. Certain situations are more conducive for written communication whereas others are better suited to verbal communication. People who are good communicators know when to use each one. These topics will be explored further in the following sections of this chapter.

Communication Skills Assessment

No one is perfect. If we were, this world would be a boring place. Below is a list of ideal qualities that should be included in the communication process. ***Think about the way you typically communicate on a daily basis at work and circle "yes" or "no" to the corresponding item.*** Be honest with yourself and afterwards you can always review the areas that you need to work on.

Verbal communication checklist

Y N   Use proper language
Y N   Speak clearly and distinctly
Y N   Use a tone and pitch that is friendly and professional
Y N   Maintain eye contact
Y N   Do not fidget or look distracted
Y N   Maintain an open and professional stance
Y N   Observe the non-verbal cues the listener is displaying
Y N   Ask clarifying questions to make sure they understand
Y N   Always open to feedback
Y N   Review follow-up items, if any

Written communication checklist

Y N   Use correct grammar, spelling, and tone
Y N   Use the correct reading level for your audience
Y N   Have a distinct introduction, body, and conclusion
Y N   Begin each communication by listing the purpose
Y N   Messages are clear and concise, getting right to the point
Y N   Stick to each major point and do not go on tangents
Y N   Link different subjects together so it has a nice flow
Y N   Highlight important or follow-up items
Y N   End with a memorable statement so they remember the point or action items
Y N   Provide an option for feedback or questions

Listening checklist

Y N   Maintain eye contact
Y N   Do not fidget or look distracted
Y N   Maintain an open and professional stance
Y N   Do not interrupt, change the subject, or think about other things

Y N   Ask questions that pertain to the subject at hand

Y N   Observe the non-verbal cues the listener is displaying (listen between the lines)

Y N   Try to make others feel at ease when they are speaking

Y N   Empathize with what they are saying to show you are listening

Y N   Show active listening by confirming what you think you heard

Y N   Respond both verbally and non-verbally to show emphasis

Verbal And Nonverbal Communication

We talk and interact with people all day. Sometimes it is over the phone, in person, through conference calls, and even video conference or webinars. It is best to choose verbal communication if you have a message that has an important subject, if you need an answer fast, if you want to persuade someone to do something, or if you need to deliver sensitive or difficult news. It is more appropriate to deliver important or formal communications at work verbally, such as a plant closing or hiring a senior level executive. Verbal communication, especially if it is face-to-face, allows the opportunity to read body language and to further build relationships. It also allows for feedback to be shared more quickly. So, if there will likely be questions as a result of the communication, it is best to deliver it verbally.

Nonverbal communication includes all of the other signs that the person is displaying, as they send a message. It is meant to enhance the spoken ideas by means of body language such as posture and facial expression, along with eye contact, tone and pitch of voice, and even proximity. For example, if someone at work runs up to you, stands real close, and speaks in a whisper, they are probably going to tell you a secret or other interesting but confidential information. You already have a general idea of what the message is about, even before they begin to speak. That is because we are always communicating, even if we are not saying anything. Many times, actions speak louder than words. For example, if you say something but your nonverbal cues do not match with your message, the person will know that you are not being sincere. In fact, not saying anything at all and standing stoically can speak volumes too. Make sure to be aware of these things when you are communicating with people.

When communicating verbally, it is important to speak clearly and distinctly so that every word is heard by everyone. Use proper language that is appropriate for the situation and the audience. Don't talk down to people because it distracts them from your message. Always maintain eye contact, do not fidget, and maintain a physical stance that shows you are interested in their feedback. That means you should not slouch, fold your arms, put your feet up, stretch, yawn, etc. In return, watch their body language and other nonverbal cues to see if they are fully interested and engaged. Ask clarifying questions to ensure they understand. For example:

- Do you get what I am trying to say?

- What do you think?

- How will you proceed with what I have asked?

Communication is rarely a one way street because there is constant feedback and follow-up. Monitoring this is an important step in the process. If the discussion is particularly important, it is always a good idea to follow up with a written communication to document the conversation, reiterate what was said, or agree upon next steps.

Written Communication

Written communication is another important aspect of any workplace. Many employees regularly prepare and/or trade email, memos, spreadsheets, forms, and procedural documents. When interacting with others, it is best to choose written communication when the information is detailed and needs to be accurately communicated. It is also more appropriate to use written communication if you need to have documentation that the communication was delivered or when you are following up on a verbal discussion. For example, if you have a verbal conversation with someone about improving their performance, meeting a deadline, or attending a meeting the next day, it is a good idea to follow up with a note.

<u>Confirmation Example 1</u>: "Jodie, thanks for agreeing to help me with the Beta Project. As we agreed, I will see you in the Operations Conference Room at 9:00 a.m. tomorrow."

<u>Confirmation Example 2</u>: "Peter, I am writing this note to document our conversation today about your job performance. Your property report was late again for the third month in a row and it is affecting our operations. You have agreed that you will complete this task on time next week and will not take anymore vacation time until it is done."

One of the most important aspects of writing is using proper spelling and grammar. No matter what you are trying to say, it will not be conveyed accurately if you do not follow proper guidelines. Next you must know your audience and choose words they can understand and relate to. Avoid incomplete or run on sentences. Don't use jargon. Make sure everything is clear and concise. Get to the point quickly but also be interesting and conversational, if the situation calls for it.

<u>Bad Example</u>: Education is important to everyone as it is to me and I am sure it is to you too. We want to give our employees an extra perk and feel it is in your best interest to educate your children so we have been thinking of ways to help you do that especially in today's troubling economy. So, we set up a tuition program that you can apply to via mail if you want your child to participate and everything about it is in the Word document that is attached to this message.

<u>Good Example</u>: The Executive Team is pleased to announce a new program that will allow our full-time employees to apply for scholarships for their children. Details are attached. Please contact me if you have any questions.

Be very careful about anything you put in writing because it can become a permanent record. Think of it this way: imagine if everything you wrote showed up on the front page of the newspaper the next day. Would you be proud or want to crawl under a rock? This often happens with email and it is easy for people to become too casual about it, especially if you consider your co-workers to be friends. Remember, it is still a business and you are there to do a job. Besides, friends at work can come and go and you never know who else might have access to your email or other work documents. The management team can legally access your work email at any time and see what you have written. It is just so easy to create and send email and that is why it is so popular. It allows you to think about what you are going to say and ensures that your ideas will be fully presented without interruptions. However, this can be addicting and make you look cold and detached if you constantly send email rather than call or speak to people face-to-face. Make sure to include a well-balanced way of communicating throughout the work day.

Listening Skills

Listening to the messages that you receive from others is just as important as creating and sending your own messages. One of the biggest mistakes people typically make in the communication process is that they do not fully listen. This can happen many different ways.

- They might have too many distractions in their environment and not be able to receive the message accurately, even if they are actively trying to

- They might not have enough knowledge about the situation or topic to be able to understand the message

- They might not be interested in the message and not even trying to listen

- They might get so excited about the topic that they immediately start forming their own thoughts in their head rather than fully listening to the other person first

- They might jump to a conclusions about what is going to be said and interrupt the person before they can finish

These are only a few examples of how the communication process can be distorted. We must remember that listening is an active process and requires more than just hearing what is said. We must listen to the words that are used, note any verbal cues that are being sent, and be able to listen between the lines. For example, some people do not have a large enough vocabulary to appropriately convey what they want to say. They may have a speech impediment or may just be having a bad day and are distracted. When this happens, the listener should read between the lines and ask follow-up questions to fill in the gaps until the message is fully understood. It is the responsibility of both the sender and receiver to make sure the communication process is working. Often we just don't spend enough time preparing what we are going to say and the message is not clear, which puts the burden on the recipient to decipher the full meaning.

Giving Presentations

Creating and giving a presentation is just another form of communication. It might involve speaking on a topic during a conference call, giving an orientation to new employees, training managers about a new product, or hosting an award ceremony. Typically it is best to set up a presentation if the information is important, detailed, or lengthy to provide. A simple phone call or email would not be enough to convey this kind of information so a presentation is scheduled. This can be advantageous to the sender of the message because they have everyone's undivided attention for a scheduled period and they have time to prepare beforehand. However, before they even begin writing their message, they should first consider the following:

1. What is the purpose of the presentation?

2. Who is the audience?

3. What is the timing?

4. What method of delivery will be used?

5. What kind of props will be used?

The first thing is to understand the purpose of the presentation. Why are you giving the presentation and what will the audience gain from it? This helps to form the title and later the opening sentences of what will be said. Knowing the purpose sets the tone and direction for the entire presentation. If you get stuck on any part of the process, you can go back to the purpose in order to guide you. The second step is to know who your audience is. For example, it may be existing managers, brand new employees, or potential clients. You must have an idea about who the recipients are before you can create a message for them. Then the next step is to be aware of the timing. You might be asked to speak for five minutes or two hours. Once you know the timeframe, it is also important to know the time of day that your presentation will be given. If it will be given in the afternoon during a lunch meeting or if it will be given at 7:00 in the evening on the last day of a week long conference, you will want to know that up front and tailor your presentation accordingly.

Now that you have information about the purpose, the audience, and the timing, you can focus on the method of delivery and determine what props to use. The method of delivery might be a conference call, a webinar, or a face to face presentation. Being able to see your audience allows for a lot more flexibility in the props that can be used. The entire situation must be taken into account when planning any kind if endeavor like this. For example, if you were asked to give a five minute speech about your latest project at the end of an internal staff meeting, it may not be appropriate to create an entire PowerPoint presentation. Alternatively, if you were asked to give a two hour presentation to a potential new client, it would probably be very boring if you just read a speech and did not use any props or other visual aids. Think about the time of day and how your audience will feel and what they will benefit most from the presentation. Be concise and make your point but also be enthusiastic and engaging. Other props you can use are photographs, diagrams, charts/graphs, poster board, handouts, videos, or even live models. You can also plan for group exercises and role play. These things can help to make your presentation more memorable.

Once you have the overall format planned, you can write the content of your presentation. It is a good idea to start with an outline that includes the title of the presentation and then each section, like chapters in a book. For example:

Title - The New Monthly Budget Procedures

1. Why we made this change

2. Why it will be good for the company

3. What they need to do including a step-by-step walk through of the new forms

4. Handout a sample completed form

5. List the troubleshooting tips and who to call if they have problems

6. Open the floor for questions

After you have created an outline, fill in the details. You might need to do research on your topic so that it is well-rounded. For example if you are training a group of people on a topic like customer service, provide some statistical facts about how other companies were more successful after receiving similar customer service training. Paint a picture of how easier their jobs will be if they follow your guidelines. Tell funny jokes about how the competition does not offer this kind of program and how bad their customer service is. Show how you want them to be different. Continually convey why the information is important and why they should be interested.

For any presentation, make sure that your opening and concluding remarks are memorable. You can open with a joke or anecdote to catch their attention. Then you can close with a more important or serious note that drives home the point of your presentation so that they will remember what you said. During the presentation, try to link each point together so that it flows. Also, practice your entire presentation several times beforehand to make sure you are within the time limits and always allow time for questions. The timing is very important because if the audience expects your presentation to end at a certain time, you will start to lose their attention after that point, especially if the following session includes a meal break. Your main goal should be to get your point across and impress them in the process so that they remain engaged and focused on what you are telling them.

Hosting And Attending Meetings

Meetings should occur regularly at every level of the organization in order to share information and keep the lines of communication open. Sometimes these meetings are one-on-one and other times they are with a group like our individual department or division. Sometimes the meetings happen across departments, like when each departmental manager gets together to share information. No matter what the situation, managers should typically check in with their staff every single day for at least five minutes. This should occur face-to-face if they are within the same building or over the phone if they are remote. This does not have to be a formal meeting, just a quick hello and how are you doing sort of thing. Managers can ask a personal question like how their weekend was and ask how a certain project at work is coming along. This lets the employee know that their manager is interested and keeping track. This also helps to build and enhance working relationships.

Besides the daily five minute individual meeting, each department should have a weekly meeting as a group. This process should allow each member of the group to speak about what they are working on.

This gives everyone a chance to share triumphs and tribulations while supporting each other in the process. If some of the employees work remotely, have them on the phone. The remote employees are often the ones who can benefit the most from team meetings. For these weekly team meetings, don't get preoccupied by too much formality. For example, you are not required to have an agenda for these meetings other than bullet points of issues to ask or discuss. It is more of an open forum for each employee to share feedback and discuss the latest issues. At any meetings like these, it is important to go around the table and allow everyone to speak. This allows everyone a turn and typically reduces the chatty people from running on too long. However if this does happen and people go off on tangents, then suggest that they discuss it offline. Alternatively, managers can assign a priority level to each project and if it is not high priority then they can agree to discuss it at another time. Weekly departmental meetings should typically take 30-60 minutes.

There should also be more in-depth meetings on a quarterly basis. These kinds of meetings are typically more strategic and focus on industry trends, how the competition is doing, or skill enhancement. These can occur intra-departmentally such as when all the marketing staff gets together or inter-departmentally such as when all directors or vice presidents meet. This might involve each department head giving a presentation, a focus on the financial status of the company and the direction it is headed, training on special topics such as new procedures or products, and may even involve outside motivational speakers. These meetings should be carefully coordinated with an agenda and a moderator should be assigned to keep everything on track. These meetings typically occur offsite and can last two to three days. These kinds of meetings may seem daunting but if they are planned and implemented properly then the attendees receive the kind of information they need to do their job successfully. After these kinds of meetings, it is a good idea to draft a communication to all of the employees to let them know the highlights and the plans moving forward. This brings everyone together as a team.

Conclusion

Having good communication skills can enhance the relationships that you have with everyone at work. Your communication skills can shape your image, allow people to give you what you want faster, and can ultimately lead to a better career. This is important because we interact with people all day at work and we are constantly sending and receiving information. When communicating with others, it is important to use proper language and to consider your audience. Another important factor is the non-verbal cues that people send when they communicate such as their posture, their tone of voice, and even the speed at which they speak. We must be aware of these things within ourselves so that we convey a complete message. We must also notice it in others as we try to decipher messages we receive.

When communicating at work, we often have the choice of doing it verbally or in writing. It is best to use verbal communication if the topic is particularly important or sensitive, if you want to persuade someone, or if you need to get an answer fast. It is best to use written communication if the topic is detailed or if you just want to document an earlier conversation. Good communicators use both forms of communication as needed based on the situation. However, one of the biggest problems with the communication process is that people do not spend enough time and effort toward listening. There may be distracters in the environment or they just might be preoccupied with their own thoughts. This is important because it is the job of both the sender and the receiver to make sure messages are transmitted accurately.

Another important form of communication occurs at work when we give presentations. When creating a presentation, the first steps to consider are: the purpose, audience, timing, method of delivery, and props before writing the content. Then create an outline before filling in the details. Once the entire presentation is complete, it is important to practice giving it so that you are comfortable and to ensure your timing is accurate. Another major aspect about communicating at work occurs in meetings. You should meet briefly with your boss everyday just to check in. Then each department should have weekly *status* meetings and quarterly *strategy* meetings. By using all of these communication tools, both yourself and those around you will work better as a team, you will be able to give your boss what he or she wants, and you will build a more professional reputation for yourself. The next chapter focuses more on your relationship with your boss and how you can become even more successful by building this mutually beneficial partnership.

Ch. 6 – Build An Alliance With Your Boss

If I have seen farther than others, it is because I was standing on the shoulder of giants. --Sir Isaac Newton

We all have a boss. No matter what our role or what company we work for, we do not work alone. However, there are no books or employee manuals on how to interact or deal with your exact boss. Each boss and each environment is unique. Having a good relationship with your boss is a primary motivator in job satisfaction and it can also reduce your stress load. Additionally, your boss can be a key supporter in helping you to achieve your long range goals. Building an alliance with your boss means that you have an agreement to seek common goals and interests. It does not only mean that you will do everything in your power to advance his or her career, but they will do the same for you. This should be a mutually beneficial relationship.

No matter what your role or position in a company, we all have someone we are accountable to. Your boss may be the supervisor of the division, a vice president, a board of directors, or even your customers. The important thing to know about your boss is this: no matter who you are, your primary job is to make your boss look good. If you make your boss look good in the eyes of others, then you will look good in the eyes of your boss. It is important for any group of people to follow the leader in order for the work to be accomplished. You may not always agree or think it is fair, but it is important to be part of the team. At work, you must put on your game face and smile. If you disagree, you should be able to voice your concerns to your boss when you are alone together, but when others are around you must present a united front. Managing the expectations of your boss is not about kissing up or being sneaky, it is about building a relationship so that everyone gets what they want, the company, the boss, and you.

What Type Of Boss Do You Have?

Do you know what your boss expects from you and what your boss values most? If not, this is your chance to learn. The most important thing you can do, especially if you have a new boss, is to learn his or her goals and then get behind them 100%. What motivates them? Is it money, power, or affiliation? How do they want to be kept informed of your progress on projects? What level of information do they want? Do they want to know details or do they want you to make the decisions and just keep them informed? It is important that you learn the basic needs of your boss in order to work alongside them. Your goal should be to become invaluable to them and help them progress in their career. Hopefully, they will take you up the corporate ladder with them.

Once you know who your boss is and what they want, adapt your style to fit theirs. For example, your boss may want the "10,000 foot view" and only want to know when a project is finished. If you are the type of person who wants a lot of direction and guidance, figure out ways to do this with limited participation from your boss or possibly seek the guidance elsewhere. On the flip side, if they like to get involved in every detail, don't take offense. Let them get involved and see your work. Over time they may loosen the reigns as they get more comfortable. As you develop a relationship, start to share your work goals with them too. Let them know what motivates you and what you want. Then you can build a mutually beneficial relationship. Everyone wants to be successful so we might as well help and support each other.

Assessing Your Boss

Think about the qualities that your boss typically displays. *For each of the following five questions, circle which of the two choices fits your boss the best:*

Q. Is your boss more of an introvert, who prefers to be alone? Or are they more extroverted and prefer to be around people? Are they chatty when you visit or do they like to get right to the work issue at hand? If they suddenly had one-hour of free time, would they spend it alone catching up on a report or interacting with others?

Introvert   Extrovert

Q. Does your boss focus more on the numbers associated with the company, such as spreadsheets, the bottom line, and profitability? Or do they focus more on the people of the company such as employee morale and customer satisfaction?

Numbers   People

Q. Is your boss more of a listener, who prefers to give and receive communication face-to-face and over the phone? Or are they more of a reader who prefers email and other written forms of communication? Which way is faster for you to get an answer? Which way do they contact you the most?

Listener   Reader

Q. Does your boss ask for details about each project you are performing or upcoming changes? Do they like to get involved in the tasks you perform? Or do they just want the highlights from a higher level viewpoint? Do they seem to get bored or frustrated if you give them too much information?

Detail-Oriented   10,000 Foot View

Q. Does your boss value people who follow the rules, such as showing up exactly on time for every meeting and making every project deadline? Or does your boss get more excited when someone shares creative ideas and thinks outside the box?

Rules   Creativity

Now that you have a brief outline of the major ways your boss functions, think of ways you can accommodate this. If they are an introverted reader, then send more email rather than calling or stopping by. If they are a numbers person and you want to present a proposal, focus more on the money that will be saved rather than how people will feel about it. If they like detail, check in with them more often and give them what they need. If they are rules oriented, make sure to comply by doing things like setting an extra reminder for yourself to attend meetings on time. Be aware of your boss's preferences and then set out to accommodate them. This is a great way to get started on improving your relationship.

Building The Relationship

Developing an effective working relationship with your boss also requires that you understand yourself. You need to know your own strengths, weaknesses, and goals so that you can adapt to theirs. For example, if you want your ideas to be heard, it is a good idea to communicate in the style your boss prefers. If you like email but they prefer face-to-face communication then you must try to accommodate them. You have a better chance of them listening to you this way anyway. Although it can be difficult to change your own style, they are the boss and they must be the ones to take the lead. On the other hand, you can't just be completely compliant and acquiesce to every single thing they want because you also need to bring fresh ideas and your unique perspective. If you don't bring something new then nothing will ever change or improve. Make sure to maintain a good balance of push and pull with your boss and never be overly argumentative or rebellious. Think of yourself as a consultant to your boss. You should give them ideas and options but it is up to them to make the ultimate decision. Once they decide, you must carry out their requests 100%.

A great way to build relationships with people is through positive and negative reinforcement. On a basic level, it is easy to understand that people will continue displaying a behavior if they get rewarded for it and they will stop displaying a behavior if they get reprimanded or punished for it. Any strong reaction, whether it is positive or negative, can reinforce a behavior. This happens at work all the time and we often don't even realize it. For example, if your boss gets upset about something and they have anger issues and yells at you about it, and then you immediately complete whatever task they just yelled at you about, then you have just taught them that yelling is a way to get you to do your job. Your reaction is reinforcing their behavior. If they get like that, you must remain calm and do not reinforce their behavior. Wait for them to calm down before reacting. You can try being very still and quiet until they have gotten it out of their system or sometimes you may need to walk away and go back later. Explain to them what you are feeling and how you can not respond when you are being treated that way. Look to actively fix the problem moving forward rather than allowing it to keep happening. On the flip side, if your boss does something that benefits you, then reward them. Find out what they like and do it for them. You can even openly make a deal. For example, "I will stay late again tonight but let me leave early next week for my son's game."

It is important to understand that almost any interaction you have can reinforce past behaviors or coach people toward new and better ones. The next time you need to spend some time with your boss but they are too busy to fit you into their schedule, offer to buy them a cup of coffee in the morning if they can meet for just ten minutes. Or find out what is making them so busy and try to take some of the burden off their hands. You don't even have to find large rewards to get their attention. Sometimes just paying them a compliment or showing your support and admiration is enough. So for example, if your boss often has problems meeting deadlines or giving you feedback on a project, when they finally do it right, heap a bunch of compliments on them, but don't be so obvious. Show how their good behavior affects you and your department in a positive light. Focus on the good and not the bad. If they get upset over something, try to wait until they are calm, and then try to work with them again. Then compliment them on their cool demeanor. You may not see a dramatic behavioral change instantly but these kinds of things require time and attention.

Remember They Are Human

No matter who your boss is, they are only human and they have strengths and weaknesses just like everyone else. A lot of people look up to their boss, even some like they looked up to their parents when they were children. There is an idealistic view that the boss is supposed to be perfect, do everything right, and be able to solve any problem that comes along. In reality, the boss is just a person like you. They might make mistakes. They might change their mind on decisions, belittle your contributions, or forget important tasks. They are all unique individuals who can get in a bad mood, make a wrong choice, and have personal problems. The key to your success is being able to navigate around these situations. Hopefully your boss has a lot of great qualities too and that is why they were promoted to a management position.

Although every boss has their unique problems, it is often easier to spot their strengths and align yourself to them. For example, if they are really good at creating big ideas, then you can approach them with problems that you can not solve and work together with them to create a fantastic idea that they will endorse. If they are particularly skilled at resource allocation, then you can go to them when you need something like technical support or marketing help. Remember to respect their time though and do not always take advantage. Make sure you give back too. Stay late when the situation requires it and assist them when they need it. On the flip side, recognize their weaknesses and plan ahead to compensate for them. They can not possibly be good at every single task. Perhaps they are all thumbs when it comes to spreadsheets or they are not very good at making speeches. Find out where they are weak and provide support in that area. You can always help them with their spreadsheets and allow them to take credit for it. You can also offer to review their speeches and give confidential feedback. Think about what you can do to make their life easier. Put yourself in their shoes. They will appreciate it, even if they don't show it right away. This will make you even more valuable to them. Along the same lines, learn what their hot buttons are. Do they get upset when someone is late for meetings? Then don't do that. Do they get upset when someone swears? Then don't do that. Do they hate to be interrupted when they are on the phone? You get the picture.

Overall, try to understand what your boss wants and needs. Recognize their preferences and try to conform to them. If they want a daily status report, give it to them. It does not necessarily mean you are deficient in this area, it just makes them happy and secure. If they just want to know the big picture, don't bother them so much with the details. If you need additional support, seek it elsewhere. If they like a specific format for a report, give it to them. You can even play around with formats and colors and test them out to see what will really knock their socks off. This will be a constant reminder to them that you are flexible and willing to accommodate them. Show your boss that *their* goals and objectives are *your* goals and objectives too. If you have a meeting to discuss "our" objectives then they will be more open about sharing their ideas and plans with you.

Managing Up

The term "managing up" does not actually mean that you have to manage your boss. However, you do have to manage the relationship and their expectations. A great overall theme to managing your relationship with your boss is to treat them as if they were a customer. This works well because we typically treat our customers like gold. For example: humor them, don't get upset, and don't let them see you sweat too much. We often have a different perspective from our boss and learning to manage up helps to manage their expectations but also allow you to voice your opinion and make an impact. This is not about manipulating the boss or kissing up. It is about achieving everyone's goals: for the company, for your boss, and for you.

There are three key themes to managing this relationship: *be honest and dependable, enjoy the journey,* and *have open communication.* The first one is pretty obvious. Always be honest and dependable when it comes to your boss and co-workers. Don't be sneaky because people see through it. They are just smart enough not to tell you to your face. Give credit to people for their ideas and never try to pass them off as your own. If you give credit to others, you make everyone look good, including yourself. Always follow the rules and honor your commitments. Also, don't go over your boss's head or behind their back to other people. This can be the kiss of death. If you make a mistake, own up to it and immediately work to get it fixed. Don't try to hide errors from the boss or sweep them under the rug. They will only snowball into larger problems and the boss will probably find out anyway. It is better if they hear it from you so that you can present a professional image and show what you are doing (or have done) to fix the problem. The main point in being honest and dependable is to follow the rules and do the right thing. Eventually it will be appreciated. These tips will also help you build a good reputation for yourself no matter where your career goes.

The second key element to managing up is to enjoy the journey. This may not seem so obvious at first but it has to do with maintaining a positive attitude and taking pride in your work. When you enjoy the process of completing your assignments, you are a happier person and will tend to spread that joy to others. One thing I have learned is that the "end result" of getting the work done is just as important as making the process of getting there enjoyable. You might be a diligent and efficient worker, but if you complain every day and make it difficult or de-motivating for others to complete their tasks, then no one will want to work with you. Try to make the process enjoyable for everyone involved, especially your boss. Tell a joke once in a while. Humor is a great tool. If you do find problems, immediately look for solutions rather than harping on the negative. There will be problems throughout our work lives because no person or situation is perfect. We can decide whether we want to just point the finger at others or if we want to be the hero and save the day. When presenting problems to the boss, try to research the issue fully and provide possible solutions before they even have to hear about it. If it is a small issue, fix it yourself and then tell your boss later so that you will get credit for it. Always respect and cherish your boss's time and try to use as little as possible. Figure out how to describe the problem and potential solutions in a clear and concise manner. Don't be offended if your boss does not go with your recommended solution, they will appreciate the time you took to present the options.

The third key element to managing up is to have open communication with your boss. Your primary goal is to be a good listener so that you understand what is expected of you. Always allow them to finish their thoughts and be an active listener by displaying open body language and attentive stature. Don't fiddle with your watch, doodle, or interrupt. Make sure to ask follow-up questions to confirm what is being asked or told to you. For example, "so you want me to take these two spreadsheets and combine them into one PowerPoint presentation that is 10-15 pages and have it ready by noon tomorrow." These are similar tips that were explained in the communication chapter but they fit equally well in this chapter also. Communication with your boss should be a two-way street. You must have basic communication skills and be able to speak and write clearly. It is important to explain exactly what you want and need and to promote your ideas and suggestions with professionalism and persuasiveness. It also often helps if you can add wit and humor. This can make it more memorable but it must always be tasteful and appropriate for the situation. When your boss tries to give you feedback, even if it may be tough to hear, push yourself to listen openly. It is very important to listen when they try to coach you toward making changes or improvements.

The following two sections provide additional tips for building an alliance with your boss:

10 Things Your Boss Wants

- ✓ Employees who are ready, willing, and able to work

- ✓ Employees who show up on time with a positive attitude

- ✓ Employees who are willing to go the extra mile without being asked

- ✓ Employees who can think outside the box and offer suggestions for improvements

- ✓ Employees who fix problems rather than just complain about them

- ✓ Employees who encourage, motivate, and support each other as a team

- ✓ Employees who keep their work area clean and organized

- ✓ Employees who take pride in doing their work correctly and without errors

- ✓ Employees who show their boss respect and appreciation

- ✓ Employees who are honest about their mistakes and do not try to cover anything up

10 Things Your Boss Hates

- ✗ Employees who stand around waiting to be told what to do

- ✗ Employees who say, "that's not my job" when someone asks for help

- ✗ Employees who are stuck in their ways and are not open to innovative changes

- ✗ Employees who exaggerate problems and do not work toward solutions

- ✗ Employees who are excessively late or absent from work

- ✗ Employees who focus too much on getting the job done quickly and make mistakes

- ✗ Employees who will not listen openly to constructive criticism

- ✗ Employees who bring their personal problems to work

- ✗ Employees who do not prioritize properly

- ✗ Employees who focus on what their co-workers are doing and not their own job

Filtering Information

Your boss can not possibly track every single task you perform and they shouldn't really have to. They should have a good basic overview of the tasks that you perform and be informed on a weekly basis of your progress. As you work with them over time, make sure to filter what you say because they do not have time to hear every single detail. If you tend to be a chatty person or an email queen, learn to give yourself "time outs" if needed. Often after several lengthy email, I give myself an email time out to allow my boss to catch his breath. I even tell him that I am doing it so that he realizes that I am making a conscious effort to respect his time. Be considerate about their position and how much information they need at the time. You might be very excited about a particular project you are working on but they might be supervising 15 projects that other people are doing too, so they probably only want to know the highlights.

A great way to filter information is to figure out how to make them successful by giving them as little work to do as possible. For example, if they ask you to perform a simple task, but you ask them 20 questions about it, then they probably could have performed the task themselves with less time and effort. If you see other people going to your boss with multiple small questions, try to assist them yourself in order to free up your boss's time. If they are a new boss or in a new situation, imagine what kind of tools or reports they might need and suggest it to them. Don't always wait for them to assign you projects and ask for things. Be proactive. If they are attending an important meeting or conference, make sure they have the reports they need. This does not mean that you should follow them around and track their every move. It just means that a little extra consideration could go a long way.

If your boss is busy, create a decision matrix on the types of things they want to give approval on and the types of things they just want to be informed about. For example, if you work in sales and your boss approves every discount you give to a client, it could be a very time consuming process for them. Be proactive and make a list of suggested rules to follow, for your boss to review and approve just once. Maybe they don't have to approve any discounts under $100 and can simply be informed via a weekly report when those kinds of discounts have occurred. This allows you both to focus more on other important tasks and could even make you look like a hero to your co-workers because they will be happy to have more empowerment over their jobs too. In summary, filter what you tell your boss so that they don't have to be involved in every detail. Learn what they want to know, what they don't want to know, what they want to be consulted on, and what they want to be informed about. Having clear processes like these can make your job more enjoyable with less time while your boss is being informed about the things they actually need to know.

Getting A Promotion Without Being Sneaky

Most people want to get promoted to higher levels of success. However, many people do not know how to go about it. Few companies have tailored career plans for each position that provide clear steps for progressing upward in the company. Wouldn't it be great of each of us were told exactly what we would have to do in order to get a promotion and a raise? For example, "to get a promotion from sales agent to sales manager, you must have a B.S. degree, three years of sales experience at this company, a certification in project management, and have maintained a closing ratio of 35% for the previous six months." If you do not have a clear career plan like this at your company, try to create one with your boss. Be honest and tell them that you want a promotion and ask what it will take to get you there. They should admire your ambition and try to help you achieve it.

The basic skills needed to get a promotion typically include minimum education requirements including additional training or certifications, minimum years of job experience, and other hard and soft skills. The hard skills may be things like advanced knowledge of Excel spreadsheets or some other software program. The soft skills may include things like effective communication and the ability to multi-task. Find out what is required at your company and then set out to achieve them. If your company is not able to provide this for you or they do not have the type of position that you aspire to, then look at the job listings posted by other companies and review their job requirements. Imagine that you are that sales manager already and conduct a job search to see what kind of skills other employers are looking for.

As you seek to attain higher levels of success, do not neglect your current position. Make sure to inform your boss when you have completed a project successfully, solved a problem, or avoided an issue from happening. It is ok to toot your own horn. Think of it as a public relations campaign for yourself and your department. You can not just make yourself look good or you could be marked as a loner. Make yourself and others around you look good and you will appear to be a successful team player and a leader. Don't overdue this but you can send an email to keep your boss in the loop. For example, send a thank you note to someone on your team for a job well done. Even better, send a thank you note to someone who helped you, from another department, and copy their boss. If you are working extra late and your boss does not realize it, send them an email so they know you are there. Don't be a total suck-up about it but make sure that your work is appreciated.

Then if you need to acquire additional skills in order to get a promotion, the best way to do this is to volunteer for extra assignments at work. It can either be an existing task that someone else already performs or it could be a suggestion for something new. Make sure that your core work responsibilities do not suffer and only take on one additional task at a time. Also make sure to fully research the task and be committed to making it a success. Don't just look for any assignment or task that no one else wants to do. Think about this strategically. If there aren't any interesting projects laying around waiting for a volunteer, then create a project. Look for ways that your department can do things better, faster, or easier. Then make a proposal to your boss about what kind of new initiative you would like to implement. If you can find ways to save time or money, you will be a hero in everyone's eyes. Of course some people will always be stuck in their ways and will not want change, but that will just make you look even better in comparison. This can also give you that extra edge over competitors when a promotion comes up. Even if you leave your company and work somewhere else, you will have this additional experience to add to your resume and impress people during future interviews.

A final step in the process to get a promotion is to network with others. You can do this with people both inside and outside your organization. Inside your organization, you can ask to attend certain meetings or simply align yourself with leaders that you admire. Your boss is not the only person at your company who can determine your success. Get to know the top managers as people and not just as co-workers or supervisors. Share common interests and seek to learn from them through that context. Make sure to attend all social events that are sponsored by your company and further build your professional reputation at those gatherings. Outside your organization, a great way to do this is to attend workshops and conferences, subscribe to trade magazines, and read books on the topics. Always keep up to date with the industry, but also keep your boss and co-workers informed. If you read an interesting article, photocopy it and pass it out to others who might be interested. This again further enhances your reputation and shows others your commitment to a chosen field.

Conclusion

No matter who you are or what your position, we all have a boss that we are held accountable to. An important part of our job is managing their expectations and maintaining a good working relationship with them. It is important to understand your boss and what their preferences, goals, and desires are. Once you understand what they want and need, accommodate them as best you can. You can use positive and negative reinforcement techniques to build the relationship and reinforce their good qualities. Remember though that they are only human and will still make mistakes from time to time. Try to focus on their good qualities and harness the benefits of those in order to advance your own career while also making them successful.

When managing their expectations, be honest and dependable, enjoy the journey, and communicate openly. This helps to build your own reputation while instilling your trust in them. It is important to make your boss look good but to do it in an honest way without being phony or kissing up. Other people will know if you are not being genuine. If you help and support your boss, especially through difficult times, they will support you and your career in return. Make sure as you are doing all of this, that you focus on yourself too. It is important to build an image and reputation for yourself so that you can progress to the next level. Always look for ways to enhance your skill set so that you will be marketable for a promotion. This also involves networking with others both inside and outside your company. Overall, you should have a positive, open, and professional relationship with your boss that is mutually beneficial. The next chapter focuses on your relationships with co-workers and provides additional tips for becoming even more successful.

Ch. 7 – Contribute To The Team's Success

The way a team plays as a whole determines its success. You may have the greatest bunch of individual stars in the world, but if they don't play together, the club won't be worth a dime. --Babe Ruth

Companies often use the word "teamwork" but few people truly know what it means to be a team player. This is something we should consider more often because we may be on several different teams at work. One team could be our own department, another team could be our branch or division, and yet another team could be our company as a whole. It takes a lot of time and patience to navigate around all of the team's needs. Being a team player means that you consider the needs of the group as a whole more than you consider your own personal needs. It is difficult to do because it means checking your ego at the door, controlling your emotions, listening more than talking, being flexible, performing any tasks you are assigned, sharing credit for the work, accepting constructive criticism from others, and providing your own feedback to others in a non-confrontational sort of way. The purpose of teamwork is to work together toward a common goal. When the team is managed well and the individuals come together to share ideas and complete tasks, anything is possible.

Here is another way of looking at teamwork. Every office or company is like a mini community just like the city or town where you live. Each employee at the company is responsible for making it run. As in every community, there are givers who make sure that areas are kept clean, supplies are stocked, people are managed, and emergency services are available in the event of a fire or other catastrophe. However, every community also has people who just expect to be handed things without making a significant contribution. These are the people who need to be catered to and do not contribute to the community outside of their core job expectations. The givers tend to take pride in their community and will do things like pick up liter even if it is not in their own backyard. The takers are typically the ones who leave the litter.

Take a hard look at yourself and determine what kind of person you are in your work community. For example, if your place of business really was a town and each person had a job within the town, what would yours be? Are you the baker who brings in sweet treats for others? Are you the fireman who volunteered to assist with the emergency evacuation procedures? Are you the cop who tells management when you see others slacking off? Maybe you are the mayor of the town who manages the overall coordination of the community? Or are you the homeless person who doesn't pay taxes? You know, the person who finds free food around the office but never brings in any themselves. These are the people who are always telling their personal problems to others but never offers to help others when they need it. Take a moment and think about what your job is in your work community. Think about the ways that job contributes to the success of others.

Benefits of Teamwork

At work, teamwork is important because your interactions with others can set the tone for the day. Being a team player allows you to build a network of individuals who will help and support you. It also improves your professional image to be seen as a team player by management. If you are not getting along with a co-worker, then you can feel stressed out just by coming to work. You might feel anxiety every time they approach you and you might even go out of your way to avoid them. This is no way to live your life and it certainly will not contribute to your career advancement. You should continually seek to build and enhance the relationships you have with co-workers. If you build and improve these relationships, you will feel more at ease at work and it makes the day go by faster. Being a good team mate can help you learn from others and expand your own job description. It can enhance your job satisfaction and reduce stress. It can also increase your value to your company and more successfully secure your career. By being a good team mate, you help promote a good reputation for yourself and develop your leadership potential.

One of the greatest benefits about being on a team is that you do not have to do all the work by yourself. Teams typically distribute the work among the members and assign tasks based on knowledge and experience. So, you can actually use your strengths and focus on your areas of expertise rather than completing every task from soup to nuts. This is nice because it really takes the pressure off. Additionally, when there is the right mix of people on a team, you can achieve great things. Each person has strengths and weaknesses and can make unique contributions to the team. As a result, more creative ideas can be formed, difficult problems can be solved, and employees can mentor each other in the process. For example, if you are on a team with someone who has great project management skills and uses a new and advanced software to keep track of the project, perhaps they could begin teaching you how to use it too. Team members can mentor each other in a variety of hard and soft skills in order to continually improve the overall quality of the team. This also helps when supporting each other. When you are on an effective team, you do not have to worry about the work piling up while you are out sick or on vacation because your team mates will help out in your absence. Being on a team also allows you to connect with people, make friends, and sometimes build life long relationships.

Team Skills Assessment

Have you ever thought about your teamwork skills? ***In the following assessment, rate your teamwork skills on a scale of 1 to 3, with 3 being the best.*** For each item that you give yourself a 3, you will later be asked to provide clear examples. Make sure to be honest with yourself and then focus on areas where you could improve.

1 – Needs improvement
2 – Adequate
3 – Above and beyond

_____ I listen to the whole story before responding or giving feedback

_____ I embrace changes in the workplace and help others to
        implement new ideas

_____ I know when I am having a bad day and I regulate myself so that I do not take it out on others by venting my problems or snapping at people

_____ I enjoy going to meetings and feel they are useful

_____ I have a reputation for being hard working and dependable

_____ When I disagree with the thoughts shared by someone else, I have no problem telling them and I do it in a non-confrontational way

_____ When I receive constructive criticism, I accept it openly without being defensive

_____ I will go along with an idea that the team agrees to, even if I do not personally agree

_____ I sacrifice my own needs for the sake of the team

_____ I am flexible when things change and work needs shift

For each area you scored a 3, provide one clear example of how you demonstrated this at work in the last 30 days. If you did not score any 3's, take your top three areas and provide examples for those:

_____

_____

_____

_____

_____

_____

Tips for Teamwork

There are many diverse aspects of creating a winning team. A lot of it has to do with the ability and willingness of the team members. However, no matter what your situation, if every member of the team follows some simple tips, the team can be even more successful. These tips for teamwork include: being cooperative, being responsible, treating others the way they want to be treated, not keeping score, and embracing different viewpoints. By remembering and implementing these five teamwork tips, you can exemplify the skills needed to be a good team member. This can make your work day easier and also improve the work quality of your team mates. These five tips will be explained further in this section.

Be cooperative

This means more than just having good manners, it is also about leaving your ego at the door, being open to new ideas, listening more than talking, being flexible as needs change, and performing any task that is assigned to you. You should also help and support your team mates as needed.

Be responsible

This is about genuinely caring about the success of the team as a whole. You should take pride in your own work, be dependable and follow through on requests, show up to meetings on time, admit when you are wrong, share the credit with your team, and accept constructive criticism from others so that you can continually make improvements.

Treat others the way they want to be treated

Don't treat others the way you want to be treated because they might not be exactly like you. Recognize their individuality along with their strengths, weaknesses, hopes, and desires. Think before you speak, pay attention to the impact your words and actions have on others, avoid personal attacks on anyone's preferences or character, focus on issues and not personalities, and treat everyone respectfully.

Don't keep score

If you go through life expecting to get back more than you give, you will always be disappointed. Don't keep track of what you are contributing versus someone else.

Focus on your own tasks and keep high standards for yourself. The overall goal should be to make the team as a whole successful and you should celebrate when that happens.

Embrace different viewpoints

It is one thing to observe and try to "tolerate" or put up with other varying viewpoints, but it is another thing entirely to fully embrace them. The world includes a lot of different people with a lot of different experiences. Recognize the unique strengths of each individual on your team, listen openly and try to put yourself in their position, and show your appreciation for their contributions.

Fun Ideas

Once you have the basics down, look for other ways to foster relationships at work. There are many ways to create a teamwork culture. You can start with the fun stuff like simply hosting a potluck lunch or having mini celebrations during the holidays. You can have an ugly sweater day or ask everyone to wear green for St. Patrick's Day. You can have an office space decorating contest for Halloween, a Bake Off contest for Valentine's Day, or a scavenger hunt to celebrate the 4th of July. You can host a barbecue almost anytime, even if it occurs indoors. You can also set up different sporting events like a softball team or golf club. The possibilities are limitless and can be based on any interests that the employees have. These do not have to be expensive or time consuming endeavors because everyone can chip in and help out.

Besides the holidays, you can have fun throughout the year with things like a book of the month club, a movie club, or a recipe club. These groups can meet during their lunch hour or other break time so that it does not interfere with their work. Many of my clients have even created their own cookbooks and given them out as favors at their holiday parties. They actually saved money rather than buying more expensive traditional favors. You can also incorporate charitable acts into these team building exercises. You can host a coat drive, food drive, or recycling initiative. If you can get the management team to agree, you could even try to plan an afternoon off, once a year or quarter, to allow the employees to participate in a charitable event. This is easy to do if you plan it to coincide with a national walk-a-thon such as for cancer awareness or diabetes. It is a great way to get the employees out of the office, building their team skills, and also doing a good deed.

These team building exercises can benefit the company also. You could host a brown bag lunch where people eat together and discuss topics. Many speakers will come in for free, like local financial planners or yoga instructors. Companies may also decide to form teams in order to solve specific problems or complete tasks like setting up a wellness committee to create national wellness programs. Employees on these committees can plan healthy contests like weight challenges, walking challenges, or smoking cessation programs. Another similar program could be an entertainment committee that plans events and reward programs across the company. These programs can help to solve company problems or to implement nationwide initiatives that may affect every region of a business. It also helps to build teamwork and leadership skills among the members of the planning team.

When teams or committees like these get together, it is a great idea to begin the meeting with an icebreaker. An icebreaker is a fun exercise that helps people relax and get to know each other better. A typical icebreaker involves grouping people into pairs and asking them to interview each other and then to share the facts about their partner to the group. However, if you put some thought into it, you could surely be more creative than that. For example, ask everyone for a fun and secret fact about themselves and type the list on a sheet and ask each person to try and match up the secret fact to the appropriate person. Host a trivia contest about the company and see who knows the most facts. You can even get physical and ask them to play games involving balls, balloons, or other fun props. Be innovative and think outside the box. It will get their creative juices flowing too. Other things to consider when hosting meetings like this are to make sure everyone is included and the tasks are divided fairly. Take notes of any items that are discussed during the meeting and distribute them to the team members afterwards. Over time, try to set up award programs for good team players so that the employees realize their hard work is appreciated and will be rewarded.

Dealing With Difficult People

When we foster positive work relationships, it makes us feel good and can reduce our stress level. However, when we have to deal with negative people, the opposite happens. Difficult people can make our blood boil. It might be a disgruntled co-worker who is having a bad day, our boss who is stressed out and ready to snap, or an angry customer who wants us to move mountains for them. We all have to deal with difficult people at one time or another. The important thing is to stay cool and not to take anything they say personally. Immunize yourself against their anger and negativity. Don't let them get you upset too or else you are just allowing the bad feelings to spread like a plague. If you let them infect you, it can cause your own productivity and overall happiness to decline. You don't deserve that. Don't let anyone else have that kind of power over you. You should be the only person in control of your emotions.

When someone is being difficult, try to make sense out of it. Put yourself in their shoes to see if you can understand where they are coming from. Sometimes it helps if you just allow them to fully vent and air their concerns. Then if you are able to help them, do it. If you are not able to help them, try to pass them off onto someone who can help them. If the relationship is important to you and your career, you might want to approach them at a later time when they are calmer to delve deeper into the issues in order to prevent the conflict from happening again. Often people try to avoid the issue or ignore that it occurred, but this will not prevent it from happening again, and that should be the ultimate goal.

Conflict Resolution Example: "Michael, are you ok? You seemed really upset earlier and I want to make sure that does not happen again. Is there anything I can do to improve the situation?"

If you are in the heat of the moment dealing with a difficult person, use these specific strategies to deal with them:

1. Listen to and validate the other person's concerns ("I understand that you are upset")

2. Find any area of agreement ("It can be very frustrating to be transferred to three different departments before someone is able to help you")

3. Acknowledge what you have heard ("But you have reached the support department now and I can address your billing problems")

4. Use descriptive communication rather than evaluative or personalized words such as "you were wrong" ("we have a ten day billing policy but since this is the first time this has occurred on your account, I can waive the late fees this time")

5. Probe for more information ("will you be able to mail in your payment before the end of the day today?")

6. Be flexible to alternate solutions ("Ok, I will type a note in the system that you will mail your bill tomorrow")

There are a variety of ways that people can be difficult, it might not always include loud or angry behavior. For example, maybe there is a co-worker who just asks a lot of annoying and repetitive questions. If you know someone like this, don't let the behavior continue, try meeting with them to discuss it. Your goal should be to eliminate or at least reduce the number of difficult people you interact with daily. If you have tried to resolve the situation but the person just won't change, then learn to cope with it. For example, if that annoying person continues to stop by your desk and ask you questions, buy yourself a bag of jelly beans or other treat and allow yourself to eat one each time they come over. Pretty soon you might actually look forward to their visits. You can use candy when dealing with other difficult people too. If someone bites your head off when you ask them a question, try bribing them with chocolate or some other treat they enjoy. Pretty soon you may become their favorite. A little charm can go a long way in dealing with difficult people.

If someone constantly needs attention from you, then try setting up a 15 or 30 minute meeting with them on a weekly or monthly basis. That way you can get their issues resolved all at once instead of piecemeal throughout each work day. If someone keeps coming to you to vent about their personal issues, try referring them to the human resource department or give them information about the employee assistance program, if your company hosts one. If someone is difficult because they are disorganized and constantly needing your reminders, then gently mention that you just received a brochure on a time management course and ask if they would like to have it. Always try to resolve the issues on your own but if you can not and the problem is distracting you from your job, then ask your boss or other co-workers for help in resolving it. Then until the problem is resolved, try to focus on your own job and don't dwell on the issue of the difficult person. Don't waste your time hating a co-worker or really anyone in your life. Chances are they don't even know that you dislike them and even if they do, they probably don't even care. So you are just wasting your time and energy on feeling all of these negative emotions for nothing. Your best bet is to focus on your own work and try not to dwell on the actions of others.

Office Gossip

Office gossip is a tremendous waste of time, reduces morale, and can potentially destroy reputations and careers. It might seem like fun to make judgments about others or share juicy stories you have heard, but spreading stories that may not be true is just plain cruel. This type of gossip happens all the time at work. One employee gets mad at someone else so they go to their friend or maybe even a supervisor to vent and maybe embellish their side of the story. If it is an actual work situation where the event occurred at work and the issue is affecting someone's ability to get their work done, then the *only* person they should go to is their immediate supervisor. Under no circumstances is it acceptable to complain or vent to another person in the office. This just wastes time and does not resolve the issue. We all know people in the office like this. They get upset at a policy change or something that someone said and they walk around to basically anyone who will listen and they tell the same story over and over. Each person who is told feels obligated to empathize, but it really just drains their energy and any happy feelings they previously had. If you do this, try to change your behavior immediately. You are in charge of stopping this no matter what side you are on in this scenario, the giver or the receiver.

If you are the receiver of the gossip and you are not their supervisor, then you are obligated to try and stop the behavior from continuing. If you do not stop it, then you are only contributing to the problem and reinforcing their behavior by giving them your attention. You may actually be making the problem worse and not better. Although it may be difficult, you should not spend any time listening to these people vent, complain, or spread negativity. As soon as they start telling you their latest sob story, let them know that you empathize but that you really do not have any power to help them and encourage them to speak to their boss or to the human resource department. Remind them that if they do not go through the proper chain of command to get the issue addressed, it probably will keep happening. If you are a member of the management team, you can inform their supervisor yourself. Either way, try to tell the person nicely that they are taking you away from your work and that they should not discuss these issues with any other co-workers either. Try to make sure they maintain their professionalism and voice all complaints through the proper chain of command.

It is not good for your career to be any kind of link in a gossip chain. A good way to prevent this from happening in the first place is to set up boundaries at work. It is certainly ok to make friends at work and foster relationships with people, but you can never allow that to interfere with your job. For example, if you are a manager and you become friends with one of your direct reports and you spend extra time with them engaging in social activities, then it can appear that you are giving them special treatment. Additionally, you should only social-ize during breaks and should not trade personal email at work. These kinds of activities take you away from completing your work and can affect your professional reputation. You should consider your time at work to be precious. Besides, the people who are difficult or who just want to vent or gossip are probably not true friends and do not deserve your time or attention anyway. The biggest whiners are probably not the people who would reciprocate if you had a problem. You can get to know the people in your office, but don't be obligated to become their therapist. Make sure to show proper manners and courtesy but don't let them invade your private space. Set boundaries and then be consistent. If someone nags you to death and you give in on their 8th attempt, then you are just reinforcing their behavior. Remember your reputation is important for your future career and you should conduct yourself professionally at all times. Besides, you never know what you might say accidentally during a gossip or venting session and your comments could always get back to the wrong people and negatively impact your career. Stay focused on your job and stay out of the gossip and rumor mill.

Rewarding Good Team Players

Everyone likes to get recognition and rewards for their hard work. We also certainly prefer working with people who are good team players, rather than people who are difficult or negative. So, we should always be looking for good team players in our environment and seek ways to encourage their behavior. When you are part of a company, you often expect the management team or big wigs upstairs to design and implement reward programs. However, the people at the top do not always recognize the contributions of the little guys. Companies do the best they can and any reward systems are great. But as any good team mate, you should look to recognize and reward your co-workers for doing a good job. If there are company programs where you can nominate an employee for a reward, like an employee of the month program, that is great. But often times you will need to take matters into your own hands.

Here are some tips to thank your co-workers and team mates for doing a good job, helping the company succeed, or for making your work life easier in some way. Try to give positive feedback and rewards to co-workers as soon as possible after the event occurs and remember to include all co-workers equitably.

- ✓ Send a thank you note to the person and copy their boss

- ✓ Write a thank you note by hand or buy a motivational card

- ✓ Have someone above you in the chain of command thank the person

- ✓ Take a photo of the person being congratulated and hang it on the wall or fridge

- ✓ For super achievers, request for them to have lunch with a senior official of the company

- ✓ Bake a special treat in their honor

- ✓ Create a unique certificate of achievement in a simple Word program and give it to them

- ✓ Hand out large gold stars to people who perform a special task

- ✓ Ask to have a special parking space designated for certain employees who excel, which can be switched up every month for a different person

Conclusion

We all spend a lot of time at work and we often spend a majority of that time working with others. Being a good team member means that we care more about the needs of the team rather than our own individual needs. This can be difficult to perform but it really is necessary in order for the team to be successful. Besides performing your assigned tasks and getting your work done, you must also contribute to the workplace community. You can contribute in your own unique ways, such as baking special items for everyone, contributing to a community candy dish, volunteering to be safety officer, or implementing a fun program like a book of the month club. Each of us is responsible for the overall success of our team and our company.

The basic tips to follow, in order to be a good team player, are to be cooperative, responsible, treat others the way they want to be treated, don't keep score, and embrace different viewpoints. This means checking your ego at the door, performing the tasks assigned to you, being respectful of others, sharing the "wins" with your team, and recognizing the strengths of your individual team mates. You can also foster team-building at work by implementing your own fun programs like coordinating a barbecue, a clothing drive, or arranging for a speaker to come during lunch. These kinds of programs can improve employee morale, foster a team culture, and sometimes even educate the employees.

Of course we all have to deal with difficult people from time to time but it is important to keep our cool and not personalize those situations. Sometimes it helps just to let them vent but we should not allow it to happen regularly, to the point of being their therapist. We have to focus on doing our own jobs and not allow ourselves to get caught up with other's negativity or general unhappiness. The same holds true for office gossip. You should not spend any of your valuable time engaged in these kinds of negative behaviors. If you set up boundaries and maintain a professional demeanor, then people will know that they can not try to spread gossip through you. On the other hand, when you witness someone performing well, it is important to give them thanks so that you are reinforcing their great behavior. These are all important skills when contributing to a team's overall success, health, and well being. If you show that the team is important to you then you will become important to your team. The following chapter focuses on another important subject which we all experience at one time or another, handling stress at work.

Ch. 8 – Handle Stress with Poise

The definition of insanity: Doing the same thing over and over again and expecting different results. --Albert Einstein

Stress is caused by your body's reaction to pressure or to change. When you are under stress, your body has a physical reaction that may involve an increased heart rate and additional hormones such as adrenaline to be created. You might breathe faster, feel tightness in your chest, or experience an upset stomach. Everyone reacts to stress differently. Sometimes, a little stress can even be good for you. For example, if you are getting ready to give a presentation and you want to do a good job, a little burst of stress can cause you to feel energized and focused. Typically though, chronic stress can cause damage both physically and mentally. Over time, ongoing stress can lead to irritability, nervousness, fatigue, insomnia, weight gain or weight loss, and depression along with a host of other problems. Chronic stress also lowers our resistance to disease and decreases our ability to work optimally. If you feel chronic stress on a daily basis then you should do something to reduce it. If you don't make any changes, then there is no reason for you to expect it to go away. In fact, the chances are better that it will get worse over time.

People are either too stressed in their life, running from one project to another, or they are not challenged enough and are stressed with boredom, repetition, and frustration. Stress can occur at work when you are not doing a job that you enjoy, that you are good at, or that challenges you. Stress can also happen when you work a lot of long hours and can not focus your attention on the things you really enjoy. This can happen when you feel torn in different directions. It can also happen more often if you don't take care of yourself with proper diet and exercise. Stress is based on your lifestyle, so that means you control it. If you do not take good care of yourself, then you can become more vulnerable to feelings of stress and the resulting health issues. The bright side is that you can take more proactive measures to prevent stress from happening in the first place.

In order to reduce the existing stress in your life, you first need to know what types of things cause you to feel stress. Everyone is different and may feel stress in different situations. For example, some people are shy and do not like to speak in front of a crowd, so they feel stress in those situations. Other people might be more gregarious and feel stress if they are left out or excluded from being able to speak. Find out what causes you stress and then work on coping with those situations to reduce the stress load. This is a very important topic because stress can affect every aspect of your health. Chronic stress can cause aging of the skin, hair loss, impotence, heart disease, stroke, and increase your chances of getting cancer. Finding a way to manage the stress in your life can make a significant impact on your well being.

Stress Assessment

Simply answer True (T) or False (F) to the 20 statements below. Then review your results and judge for yourself if you need to make changes in your life to reduce stress.

_____ My job responsibilities are clear and I understand my role here

_____ I am fully on track to achieve all of my career goals

_____ I always meet my deadlines

_____ I don't mind staying late once in a while when the workload increases

_____ When my energy is low, I know how to boost it without drugs or caffeine

_____ I rarely watch the clock and anticipate closing time

_____ I spend a little time everyday alone with my thoughts or feeling relaxed

_____ I am seldom distracted or moody

_____ I know what my hot buttons are and what causes me stress

_____ When I feel agitated, I know how to quickly calm and sooth myself

_____ I use stress relieving techniques like going for a walk or taking a drive

_____ I never feel like I need to raise my voice to be heard at work

_____ People never raise their voice at me in anger or frustration

_____ I am able to recognize when someone else is upset

_____ I easily let go of my anger

_____ People can not easily push my buttons and make me upset

_____ I can count on people in my personal life to listen to me when I need to vent

_____ I fall asleep and stay asleep easily without thinking about work

_____ My priorities are in order

_____ My family/friends never complain that I spend too much time focused on work

What Is Stress?

Our lives are full of expectations, deadlines, responsibility, and accountability. Along with that comes stress. If you frequently feel frazzled, crazed, or even panicked, then it is time to focus on getting your nervous system back into balance. You must first learn to recognize the symptoms of stress and then try to combat them. Everyone reacts differently to stress because everyone has unique personalities and backgrounds. For example, some people embrace change whereas others can be frozen in fear by it. A major factor of stress is what you think about the situation and how much time you spend worrying about it. This goes back to the chapter on positive attitude and the "scripts" we have running through our heads. You are in charge of how you feel and should not allow stress to take control over your thoughts or emotions. For example, when you are in traffic, do you get upset and angry, gripping the steering wheel, and yell at people while you keep thinking about how late you are going to be? Or do you breathe deeply, listen to soothing music, and keep your cool?

When you are under any kind of stress, your nervous system responds by releasing hormones into your blood stream. These may include adrenaline and cortisol. Hormones like these get your body ready for action by increasing your heart rate and tightening your muscles which makes you breathe faster and sharpens your senses. This increases your stamina and your reaction time. Back in our prehistoric days, this kind of response would benefit us because in the eyes of danger we would quickly have to determine whether to "fight or flight." It was our body's way of protecting us. Today, we rarely experience danger that extreme. So now the intense emotions we feel under stress often cause us more harm than good. One way to cope with this problem in modern times is to know what causes us stress and being able to respond to those situations appropriately. It is important to be in tune with your body and to recognize when it is under stress. The signs and symptoms of stress vary by person but it can affect the mind, body, and behavior in a variety of ways. A comprehensive list of symptoms that *may* be associated with stress is provided below.

*Please remember to consult your doctor if you have any ongoing health problems or symptoms.

Physical symptoms of stress

- Aches and pains in the body

- Headaches or migraines

- Diarrhea or constipation

- Irritable bowel syndrome or ulcers

- Nausea or dizziness

- Chest pain or rapid heart beat

- Loss of sex drive

- Frequent coughs/colds/flues

Behavioral symptoms of stress

- Eating more or less (weight gain or loss)
- Nightmares or other sleep disturbances
- Isolating yourself from others
- Unusual clumsiness such as tripping or dropping things
- Being sensitive to loud noises or bright lights
- Developing new allergies
- Procrastinating or neglecting responsibilities
- Using alcohol, cigarettes, or other drugs to relax
- Displaying other nervous habits such as nail biting or pacing

Emotional symptoms of stress

- Moodiness
- Forgetfulness
- Irritability or short temper
- Feeling overwhelmed
- Sense of loneliness or isolation
- Depression or general unhappiness
- Bewilderment or confusion
- Obsessive or compulsive behaviors such as repetitive hand washing

Cognitive symptoms of stress

- Memory problems

- Inability to concentrate

- Poor judgment

- Seeing only the negative

- Anxious or racing thoughts

- Constant worrying

The most dangerous part of stress is how easily it can creep up on you. If stress builds up slowly over time, most people just get used to it. Many people even believe that they thrive on it. It starts to feel familiar or even normal. In fact, some people get so used to it that they can't seem to function unless there is a lot of stress going on around them. It is like they create the chaos in order to keep their senses stimulated. Perhaps you know someone like this? Stress is a very serious issue that can cause a lot of damage so it is important to know your limits. When was the last time you had your blood pressure checked? You should get a physical every year and can even get your blood pressure checked at other times such as at the dentist office or gynecologist appointments. You can also purchase a home testing kit to regulate it more frequently. This can be particularly helpful because after several tests, you will get a better feel of when you are under stress and what kinds of situations cause it.

What Specifically Stresses You Out?

The potential causes of stress vary by person. For example, some people like having the control of driving to work while others prefer to read a book or relax on public transportation. Some people like to be in a leadership position where they can manage people or systems, whereas others would be very uncomfortable and nervous if they were put in charge. Any situation can stress someone out, even a positive event. For example, it may feel great to win an award at work, but it can still fill your stomach with butterflies to step up on a stage to receive it in front of everyone. Your internal thoughts about any situation at work can potentially cause you stress too. People who have a negative attitude, are generally pessimistic, have unrealistic expectations, fear change, or are inflexible or intolerant are generally going to be more susceptible to stress. Environmental factors at work can also be more conducive to stress such as unclear job descriptions, inadequate training, or poor communication. The potential causes of stress are everywhere.

So, look around your work environment and think about the last seven days. What caused you stress at work over this last week? Make a list of items, even if they initially seem minor. If you can't think of anything, start keeping a log. When a certain person or event causes you to feel stress or any of the stress related symptoms mentioned previously, write it down. You can even attach a stress level score to each event. Once you recognize the symptoms and then link them to the stress causing event, you are halfway toward solving the problem. Don't avoid this exercise because it is critical to improving your overall health. The goal is to find out what triggers you into feeling stress and then later on developing coping mechanisms to deal with the stress. So, after keeping the log, evaluate the list. See if there are any trends and categorize the items by the things you can control and the things you can not control. Then focus on changing the stressors that you can control and learn to cope with the ones you can not control.

Your specific stressors could involve a variety of things. Perhaps it is just completing all of your various work assignments on time. Perhaps it is the pressure your boss is putting on you to create a certain lengthy report. Perhaps you are putting pressure on yourself by volunteering for a lot of projects at once. Sometimes it is a particular person in our work life who causes us stress because of their attitude or lack of professionalism toward us. Some of these things you can control and some things you can not. However, it will never be possible to remove all the stress from your life. We can not control everything that goes on around us. Certain factors also affect your tolerance level to stress. For example, if you have a strong support network of family and friends who can help you through difficult periods, then your stress level will probably be lower. If that support network changes or diminishes, then your stress level may increase and the number of stressors in your life may increase as a result. Always keep track of the stressors in your life so that you can continually find ways to combat and reduce them.

Here is an example of a stress log that you can use to keep track of the stressors in your life along with a stress rating scale. *Use this as a sample and create your own stress log for the last week or month.*

Date	Time	Incident	Stress Symptoms	Rating (1-10)
4/22	10:35	A client called to cancel an account. She said that no one had returned her calls for days and I assured her that no one from my department had received any messages from her. She got upset and yelled at me. Now we have lost the business.	My heart was beating fast and I felt warm and a little dizzy.	8
4/25	3:45	A co-worker came to me upset about a personal problem and cried while telling me.	I felt sad and a little helpless.	5

How To Reduce Your Stress

There are two ways to reduce stress in your life: proactively and reactively. Being proactive means that you take steps to reduce stress before it occurs. Being reactive has to do with how you deal with stress in the moment it happens. These topics will be discussed further in this section. Being proactive about reducing stress in your life can include implementing healthy habits like maintaining a proper diet, exercising regularly, and taking time for yourself each day to reflect and relax. These kinds of things can reduce your overall stress level and enhance your general feelings of well being. Then when a stressful event occurs, it may not seem as bad. Below are some quick tips on preventing stress proactively.

Proactive measures to reduce stress before it happens:

- ✓ Eat healthy

- ✓ Exercise regularly

- ✓ Take yoga classes

- ✓ Learn how to meditate

- ✓ Plan time for yourself each day to think and relax

- ✓ Maintain a flexible and open schedule (don't book too much at once)

- ✓ Add humor to each day

If you want to be proactive about controlling stress in your life, a great way to do it is to always try to have balance. Make time to do the things you love. Do not be hyper focused on only one thing or you could lose track of what matters most to you. Take time to smell the roses and enjoy life. Keep your priorities in check. On a personal level, money is a big source of stress so make sure to have a budget and stick to it. Always put a little money aside for a rainy day. Find your passion and spend time doing things that you enjoy. Focus on a hobby or volunteer work. Develop your communication skills because it will allow you to articulate what you are feeling, what is frustrating you, and what you need to change. Having good organizational skills can help the same way in this respect. By being organized, having everything in its place, and following a schedule clearly, you can reduce a lot of problems that cause stress.

On the other hand, being reactive to stress involves knowing when it is happening to you in the moment, reading the signs and symptoms, and having quick on the spot remedies to reduce, remove, combat, or cope with it. If the situation is something you can control then you should try to do just that. For example, if you are often stressed because you arrive late to work in the morning, then change your habits so that you can wake up earlier and have more time. However, if the situation is something you can't control, like the annoying behavior of a particular co-worker, then learn to cope with it. Below are some quick tips on reducing stress in the moment.

Reactive measure to cope with stress in the moment it happens:

- ✓ Breathing exercises

- ✓ Count to ten (or higher if the situation requires it)

- ✓ Walk around the building

- ✓ Run up and down the stairs if you need to expel more energy

- ✓ Drive to a scenic place for lunch or arrange to have lunch with a friend

- ✓ Sing a song (it stabilizes your breathing while expending nervous energy)

- ✓ Search the internet for a pleasant picture and focus on it for five minutes

✓ Do a good deed for someone else because it can make you feel good

✓ Call the Employee Assistance Program (EAP) if your company sponsors one

Try to look at each situation objectively. If someone is yelling at you, think about how out of control they are with their emotions. Look at how poised you are in contrast. Perhaps they have major issues going on in their life whereas yours is pretty good. Try to communicate calmly during any stressful situation without becoming angry or defensive. State the facts and explain how the stress is affecting you.

<u>Stress Resolution Example</u>: "I understand that you are upset because you were not invited to the meeting, but I was not the one who scheduled the meeting, and I don't appreciate being yelled at."

Typically, if there is nothing you can do to control the stressful situation, then it is best to excuse yourself and walk away. This way you do not react until you have calmed down. Taking a walk allows you to get away from the immediate environment that is causing the stress and allows you to expel energy. It also gives you the benefit of physical exercise and burning calories. Deep breathing works well to reduce your heart rate if you feel it has increased. This can be as simple as taking deep breaths and holding them for a few seconds before exhaling completely. These are just a few tips to perform in the moment. However, managing stress is really about taking charge of your own emotions and reactions. Always be in charge of your thoughts, emotions, and the way you respond to problems. If you implement just a few of these stress management techniques, it can lead to a much healthier and more productive work life.

Develop A Personalized Action Plan For Reducing Stress

Now you know more about what stress is and what your specific symptoms are when you are under stress. If you maintained a stress log then you have identified specific situations that stress you out. You also have some general ideas on how to reduce the kinds of stress that you are exposed to. The next step is to create a personalized action plan for reducing stress in your life. Select one of the situations from your stress log that caused you to feel stress in the last week. It can be hard to pick which one, but choose one that caused a moderate level of stress. This way it is challenging but not overwhelming. You can build up success and confidence before tackling larger challenges. This is a particularly good exercise if you have high blood pressure, if you get upset easily at work, or if you ever get hot under the collar and yell or snap at people. Take time now to figure out why you react this way. Then you can make a list of stress management techniques that work the best for you and you can refer back to the list as needed. You can tailor your action plan any way you would like. The following one is provided as an example.

Sample Personalized Action Plan

I.   NOTES FROM STRESSFUL EVENTS THAT HAVE
       OCCURRED

<u>Stressful event sample # 1:</u>
On a Wednesday morning, a client called to cancel an account. She said that no one had returned her calls for days and I assured her that no one from my department had received any messages from her. She got upset and yelled at me. Now we have lost the business.

<u>What were the circumstances?</u>
I did not get any additional information but she was probably leaving messages with another department and they did not forward them to us.

<u>What was your reaction?</u>
I was very upset and defensive. My heart was beating fast, my face was flushed and red, and I felt very warm. I was also embarrassed that my co-workers could hear the argument.

<u>What, if anything, was surprising?</u>
I don't usually get that upset when someone is mad at me but
I was concerned about losing such a large account.

<u>What bothers you the most about it?</u>
The biggest fear I had during the conversation was thinking
about what my boss was going to do when she finds out. I still
have not told her yet and have a lot of anxiety about having to
do that.

<u>What kind of strategy could you use moving forward for
situations like this?</u>
I should have tried to keep her on the phone longer so that
I could explain. I was so upset, I just couldn't wait for the
conversation to end. Also, I could try to call her back and
straighten things out. I could probably also find out who she
actually left the message for and ask why they did not forward
it.

<u>What do you want to change?</u>
I think I am just stressed out over money right now and
was overly upset when she threatened to take her business
away. I am going to speak to my boss about taking an
assertive communication course so that I can deal with angry
customers more easily and so that I feel more comfortable
with confronting co-workers. I might also look into a savings
fund to put some extra money away so if any other clients
cancel their account, I won't be so strapped for cash.

II.   STRESSORS I WANT TO ADDRESS IN THE FUTURE

<u>What is the stressor?</u>
Angry clients

<u>What is my goal?</u>
I need to communicate with them better when they present
their problems to me.

<u>What roadblocks might hinder my success?</u>
The roadblock is my own feelings of insecurity. I was never able to assert myself before.

<u>The following supporting factors are:</u>
My boss wants me to get better at this and I know she would support my efforts. My co-worker Stacy is good at this skill so maybe she will teach me a few tips. I will ask her tomorrow.

III.   STRESS MANAGEMENT TECHNIQUES

<u>Sample 1 – Breathing exercises</u>
I tried this on May 14 when my boss was angry with me but she was still in the room and just gave me a funny look. I need to try this when I am alone.

<u>Sample 2 – Taking a walk</u>
I tried this last week but it was raining and just made me more depressed. Do this one only in nice weather or drive to that indoor track across town, if there is time.

<u>Sample 3 – Running up and down stairs</u>
I tried and liked this one. It helped me release my anger and I did it until I was tired. Afterwards I felt more relaxed physically but I was also energized emotionally.

<u>Sample 4 – Do a good deed for someone</u>
I have not done this yet but I plan to write Jim a thank you note for helping me last week. I want to think of more suggestions for this category too.

Conclusion

Stress is a factor of life and you will definitely experience it at one time or another. Sometimes stress is a good thing because it keeps you alert and energized. But beyond a certain point, experiencing too much stress can cause damage to your health, your productivity at work, your relationships with others, and your entire quality of life in general. Long term exposure to stress can lead to serious health problems. Chronic stress can disrupt nearly every system in your body. It can raise blood pressure, suppress the immune system, increase the risk of heart attack and stroke, contribute to infertility, and speed up the aging process. Long term stress can even rewire the brain, leaving you more vulnerable to anxiety and depression in the long run. As a responsible employee, you should recognize your own symptoms of stress and pay attention to what your body is telling you. You should also take time for yourself to relax and reflect, smell the roses, recognize beauty, and celebrate accomplishments.

The important thing about managing your stress is knowing how much stress you are under and recognizing the particular people and situations that stress you out. Stress can be caused by internal factors like your ability be flexible toward change and your feelings of being in control of your life. The external factors are things like angry clients or rude co-workers. If the factor is external and you can't control it, then you need to learn how to cope with it. There are proactive ways to reduce stress in general and they typically include living a healthy and well balanced life. There are also reactive ways of dealing with stress in the moment such as taking a walk and breathing exercises. Many of us have heard these things before but we do not practice them regularly in our work lives. Once you have an idea of your specific symptoms of stress, the specific stressors in your environment, and the specific stress techniques that work best for you, then you are well on the road to leading a better life. The next chapter expands on this and explains how to have full work/life balance.

Ch. 9 – Maintain Work/Life Balance

I know God will not give me anything I can't handle. I just wish that He didn't trust me so much. --Mother Teresa

Having work/life balance means that you spend your time wisely on both work and personal activities. There is no exact formula for maintaining balance because we each have unique lives. What may be the right balance for one person may not be the same for another. Additionally, although you may have good balance now, your needs may change over time. A quick way to know if you have balance in your life is to assess whether you experience both achievement and enjoyment in your professional and personal life. On the other hand, if you often feel stressed, overwhelmed, torn in different directions, or if your family or friends complain that you do not give them enough attention, then you might not be in balance. You might also be out of balance if you simply do not spend enough time nurturing yourself and cultivating your own hopes and dreams.

Everyone has some kind of life outside of work, whether it is with family and friends, engaging in charity work, going to the gym or participating in sports, enjoying a hobby, or pursuing spiritual endeavors, just to name a few. We also have regular ongoing chores that we typically have to perform like food shopping, laundry, dry cleaning, dentist appointments, and paying bills. We derive satisfaction from the many roles we assume but the demands can often overlap and conflict. When the demands of one role make it difficult for us to satisfy the demands or obligations of something else, we can become frustrated, upset, and stressed. In order to prevent this from happening on a regular basis, we have to fully understand and manage the expectations of others. For example, we can not tell our boss that we will work late every night and also tell our significant other that we will be home on time for dinner every night. We must make sure the people in our lives have reasonable expectations and then we must be consistent in meeting those expectations. We also need time to relax, enjoy ourselves, and rest.

So, do you strive to maintain balance in your life? Do you consciously spend your time on the things that matter the most or do you allow yourself to get pulled into whatever direction the environment dictates? It is up to you about how and where you want to focus your time and energy. We each have 24 hours a day or 1,440 minutes to spend. Once that time is used, it is gone. So, we need to spend it wisely. Most importantly, know that life does not balance itself. Maintaining balance is an ongoing process. Your needs and values will change over time so you must constantly evaluate where you are spending your time and if you need to make changes or adjustments. Understanding this can help reduce your frustration and help you to take more control of your life. The goal should be to work optimally in a job you love, have time for friends/family, be able to do enjoyable things like play golf or take dance lessons, and also have time to just relax at least a few moments each day.

Work/Life Balance Assessment

Multiple Choice: Circle the answer that best explains your current situation.
Remember, no one is perfect and there is no perfect score. Review your answers and decide for yourself if you want to make any changes to be more in balance.

1. Do you maintain a schedule?
    A. I don't have any kind of schedule and my life gets chaotic sometimes
    B. I don't have any kind of schedule, but I like to take things as they come
    C. I have a schedule and stick to it most of the time
    D. I have a schedule and I always stick to it

2. Are you on track to achieve your goals?
    A. I don't have any specific goals at this time
    B. I have goals but I am not pursuing them at this time

C. I am on track to achieve some of my goals

D. I am on track to achieve all of my goals

3. Do you know when you are out of balance?

A. I don't know when I am out of balance

B. I know when I am out of balance but I can't do anything to change it

C. I know when I am out of balance and sometimes I can get back on track

D. I know when I am out of balance and I can always get back on track

4. Do you bring work home?

A. I bring work home and my friends/family don't like it

B. I bring work home occasionally but my family/friends don't mind

C. I don't bring work home but sometimes it piles up in the office

D. I don't bring work home because I am able to get it all done at the office

5. Do you spend your time the way you want?

A. I do not generally spend my time the way I want because others in my life dictate where I am needed most

B. I don't spend time the way I want on a daily basis but I try to schedule important things occasionally

C. I generally spend time the way I want but sometimes other priorities or tasks get in the way

D. I have clear goals and boundaries so that I can spend my time how I want

What Is Work/Life Balance?

Everyone needs to have balance in their lives. We all struggle to balance our careers, our families, our health, our emotions, our social lives, and our spirituality. We can all think of instances in our life when we have spent too much time in one area, only to have another area suffer. A particular area of concern is usually between our work and family. Although our family is typically the most important thing to us, our job is what pays the bills, which in turn maintains our family life, so we have to be extra careful in balancing these two. It is not like we can divide our time equally 50/50 on each task. There is no easy formula. Work/life balance is more about giving enough time to each task or obligation so that each person in our life is happy and so that we feel a sense of achievement and enjoyment within ourselves. We can feel this in many areas of our life, based on our needs at the time. However, over time, those needs will change. Staying in balance requires that we are flexible toward the demands of our environment and to our own personal needs.

It is easy to get out of balance because we all have unique obligations and interests. We have a multitude of choices every day on how to spend our time and although that is a great thing, it can be tough to decide where to put our focus. Typically when we are out of balance, we reduce or eliminate the things that are easiest to control, like having fun, exercising, or relaxing. However, these are important parts of life that helps keep us sane and actually allows us to be happy and productive people. Besides, there is no easy way out when it comes to balancing your life. If something is important to you, like staying healthy and exercising regularly, then you should try to make time for it. Often having balance is about time management and setting personal boundaries. This way we are managing expectations and we don't have to go back later and follow-up or fix mistakes. A little planning and preparation can go a long way with maintaining balance. The primary goal is to make conscious choices about how we spend our time. You must find balance in your life to determine where you are now and where you want to be moving forward. You must also remain flexible to the changes in life so that you can re-balance and shift priorities as needed.

Benefits Of Having Work/Life Balance

People who live balanced lives learn to evaluate priorities and focus on the big picture. They understand the difference between quality and quantity when it comes to time and they dedicate quality to the things that matter most. We can't just be parents, employees, and members of the community. We have to be loving parents, dedicated employees, and upstanding members of the community. We need to live our lives with passion and with purpose. By maintaining balance, everyone will feel like they are a priority to us. Additionally, people in balance lead healthy and well rounded lives. They are in shape both physically and mentally, they are productive employees at work, they have good relationships with family/friends, and they typically also have hobbies or other interests where they are able to dedicate some time. They feel more like whole and complete people with well-rounded interests. Life is more exciting and enriching this way.

People in balance have structure and make both short term and long term plans. They know how to prioritize and accommodate conflicting demands. They also know when to commit to something and when to decline or refuse pending obligations. This way they do not take on too much at once. People in balance notice the warning signs when their balance is shifting and one area of their life is infringing on another. They also know tools and strategies for making changes so that the balance re-shifts in their favor. People in balance always make time to be alone with their thoughts to reflect, plan, rejuvenate, or just plain relax. They know that a good balance involves both work and play. People in balance have a positive attitude and feel fulfilled. They not only have goals, but are on track toward completing them. They value open communication and know how to shift gears and refocus when needed. These are the people we look up to because it seems like they have it all.

Time Log

In order to determine your own balance, you need to take an inventory of everything that is important in your life and then track how much time you actually spend on each one. Do this exercise for yourself right now. There are 168 hours in a week and most of it is spent sleeping, eating, and working. ***Calculate how much time you spend on each major activity in your life.*** Keep in mind that if you spend eight hours per night sleeping and eight hours per day working, plus spending time on your commute, eating, and chores, then you will have very little time leftover for any other activities. In your log, calculate the total hours you spend at work, including your commute time to and from work. Then for the following week you can break that down even further and track exactly how you are spending your time at work. For example, when you are at work, how much time do you spend socializing and sharing stories? How often do you allow distractions to interfere with your plans? Complete the log below and judge for yourself.

Activity	Hours Per Week
1. Sleeping	
2. Eating	
3. Total Time Working (including your commute time)	
A. Checking Email	
B. Phone Calls	
C. Meetings	
D. Creating Reports	
E. Distractions	
F. Miscellaneous	
4. Family	
5. Friends	
6. Chores	
7. Charity Work	
8. Exercising	
9. Hobbies	
10. Watching Television	

Total = 168 Hours

Once you record the hours you have each week and the ways you actually spend them, you will be able to see if you can make changes or not. Sometimes, you may feel guilty in one area because other priorities are taking up your time but you have to let that go. For example, if you only get to see an extended family member once a month or a few times a year and you do that because you are focusing on other priorities, then don't feel guilty about it. Let it go and focus your energy in more positive ways. Then when you do see that family member, shut out all other distractions and focus on giving them quality time and attention while you are together. Sometimes, this can be more meaningful to them than a larger quantity of time spent when you are distracted by other things.

The Balancing Act

There are many tools that you can use to help find your balance. Everyone has unique problems they must cope with and navigate through, but there are some simple tips that can help most people. The five key tips to focus on, in order to have more balance in your life, are: to create a schedule, set boundaries, compartmentalize, reduce clutter and waste, and make time for yourself. These five areas will be explained further in this section. Many other chapters of this book provided tips that can also be used toward maintaining balance, like time management, organizational skills, setting goals, coping with stress, and communicating openly. These skills can be applied toward your ultimate goal of being in balance.

Create a schedule

Most people have some sort of schedule to their lives, even if it is not clearly written. For example, you probably wake up at a certain time each morning, have to be at work by a certain time, and you probably take a meal break at a certain time. It is good to have this kind of structure and routine in our lives so that we know what is expected of us and where we need to be. This also allows others to know when they can depend on us. It can be helpful to incorporate this kind of structure into our personal lives too. For example, create certain times that you go to the gym, go to church, or simply help your kids with their homework. You can even create special nights, like maybe every Tuesday is game night with your children and every Thursday is date night with your spouse. By setting general guidelines like these, you can schedule your other tasks around them. Having a schedule also allows you to plan your day and make decisions about your time and attention more quickly and easily.

Set boundaries

Once you create a schedule, make it known to the important people in your life. This is the first step toward creating boundaries. For example, if you have a gym night and a date night, let your boss know and explain that you will be happy to work late on alternative evenings. Then when various people make requests to you, learn to say "no" without guilt. It is OK if you can't do it all. For example, don't volunteer for every assignment at work plus promise to direct a school play. You will just disappoint people if you take on more than you can truly handle. Also, don't do things out of guilt. If you are living life in balance then you shouldn't feel guilty. If you have a schedule and your priorities are in order, the important people in your life will better understand the choices you make. Of course be ready to make changes if any emergency situations arrive, but try to stay committed to your promises if you can. Setting boundaries can involve turning off your cell phone when you are with family or friends. Alternatively, when you are at work, you should not receive excessive personal calls and email because it can distract you from your job. Think of other ways to set boundaries in your life and then communicate the importance of them to the people closest to you.

Compartmentalize

When you compartmentalize the tasks you perform, it means that you separate them and focus on each one at a time. By giving your exclusive and undivided attention on each task, you can get the job done more quickly and with fewer errors. This is not always possible due to our busy jobs and conflicting personal demands, but generally it can work well in most situations. For example, if you are at work, then stay focused on your work and don't get sidetracked by distractions. If you need to take a break, try to remove yourself completely so that you can relax. It is not really a break if you keep checking your email. No matter how much you are passionate about your job, ultimately you need to be able to "turn it off" once in a while and power down so that your batteries can recharge. This also helps you to take a step back and see things more clearly. If you are with your family or friends, try to focus on them exclusively and don't take business calls or get distracted by work unless you really have to. Also, when you are between tasks, like driving home from work, take time to shift your focus so that you are leaving work thoughts at work and can exclusively focus on your family when you get home. Always stay focused and add quality attention to each task you perform.

Reduce clutter and waste
Take a fresh look at your work, car, and home environment. Then remove, reduce, or delegate things that are not causing fulfillment in your life. For example, start with your physical space. Do you have a lot of knick knacks that you are constantly dusting at work on your desk or throughout your home? Put them in a nice cabinet, storage bin, or just throw them away. The busier you are, the more important it is to simplify your life. The less stuff you have means the less stuff you have to clean. This is not just about physical objects. You can do the same thing with the tasks that you perform. Is every task that you perform (both at work and at home) mandatory and does it give you fulfillment and job satisfaction? If you would rather focus on other more important things, see if you can delegate the lower level or less interesting tasks to someone else. If not, maybe you could perform them more efficiently or maybe not at all. At work, run an audit on your duties to see if your company still needs you to perform the same exact thing everyday. At home, consider hiring a cleaning service to come once a week or pay a neighborhood kid to cut the grass so that you have more quality time to spend with family and friends.

Make time for yourself
Always make time for yourself. Try to set aside at least 15 minutes a day to be alone to relax, think, or do something you enjoy. If you are

already super busy then you can try to use this time during your commute to and from work, during your lunch hour, or in the evening after the kids go to bed. Unwind after a crazy day at work by reading in bed, taking a hot bath, going to the gym, or even just taking a walk. These activities will help keep you calm and centered which can enhance your performance in other areas of your life. Plan ahead for fun activities like getting a massage or taking a vacation. Then you have something to look forward to. Also, try new things. This helps spark your interest and creativity and also allows you to be more well-rounded. Play golf, go to the arcade, learn a new game of cards, anything to keep you stimulated. If you think it is selfish to spend time on your own personal needs, then you are wrong. If we neglect our own needs or continually put them aside then we will suffer as a result. We must reserve some time and energy to care for our own personal needs in order to maintain balance in our lives. Identify your individual needs whether it is physical, mental, emotional, or spiritual and then find ways to satisfy them.

Shifting Time In Your Schedule

If you already follow the other ideas listed here and you still have trouble getting everything done, then you need to look for ways to adjust the time in your schedule. Many people think this is about "finding" time, but that is not the case because the time was never lost. You have the same amount of time to spend everyday. It just requires a careful analysis about what you are doing with it and what you are willing to change. For example, if someone continually complains that you are not giving them enough attention then you either need to make a change or sit down and talk to that person and let them know you are already giving them as much as you can. If you want to get real fancy about this, you can look back at your time log, and then rank order each task you perform based on its importance to you. Label #1 next to the most important task that you perform and then work your way down the list. Then go back and look to see if the amount of minutes you spend on each activity coincides with the ranking. For example, watching television may be low on your list of priorities but you might spend several hours per week doing it. Perhaps this is one task that you can cut back on so that you can focus more on other areas? Or you can try to combine the tasks. If you want to spend more time with family and friends but you like to watch television, try hosting a movie night or other fun event.

If you have problems multi-tasking or maintaining a schedule, then ask your friends, family, or co-workers for help. Listen to their feedback because they know you best. If both your family and your boss tell you that you work too much, then take the hint. You might not need to stay in the office until 7:00 or 8:00 every single night. If you have problems finishing tasks, ask others for help. If you have more chores than others in your house, try delegating more. If you do more at work than someone else who has the same job description, ask your boss what you can do to get a more manageable workload. Keep in mind the rank order of your priorities and make those your ultimate goal. You won't be able to accommodate everyone but you may see common themes if you ask them for their feedback. Most importantly, be honest with yourself. No one is perfect so you must look at your life objectively and decide if you are doing things optimally or if something needs to change. If you regularly perform a task that is stressing you out or draining you of your energy, look for support or try to delegate it to someone else. No one else expects you to be a super hero so you should not expect that from yourself either.

So, are you happy where you are now or do you want to commit more time to your job so that you can get ahead and be promoted? Or do you feel like you are spending too much time at work and want to focus more on your kids? Or do you feel pulled in a lot of directions and you do not have enough "me" time? Think about what your priorities are and if you are living the life you want. Achieving balance is an ongoing process that requires regular attention and reflection. Remember that you don't have to reinvent the wheel every time an obstacle gets thrown at you. As you try to maintain your own balance, remember to keep things in perspective. See the big picture and don't let minor upsets ruin your outlook. Keeping things in perspective means that you continue to focus on what really matters. You might want to have money and security but most people would not sacrifice their health or even their enjoyment of life as a result. Don't take yourself too seriously and remember to see the lighter and brighter side of things.

What To Do If You Get Out Of Balance

In our hectic world, we tend to respond to the most immediate or pressing issues even though they may not be the most important to us. Unfortunately, it is usually the squeaky wheel that gets the grease. Sometimes we even react to circumstances and situations without thinking or fully planning first. For example, we often overextend ourselves by making too many promises. Although our intentions are good because we just want to please the people in our life, these actions can throw our balance off. Sometimes we feel out of balance because we allow our behavior to be dictated by external circumstances rather than by internal values and choices. This happens when we begrudgingly agree to perform a task but do it through gritted teeth while we wish we were somewhere else.

To restore balance in our lives, we must make a conscious choice to act in accordance with our values rather than react to external circumstances. We must stay in control and be proactive about our schedule rather than reactive to circumstances. We are often our own worst enemies, placing undue pressure on ourselves to do everything perfectly, but we must realize that no one is perfect. Demanding perfection from ourselves or others is unrealistic and often leads to disappointment. Rather than expect perfection, make your expectations realistic and attainable. After you acknowledge your limitations, give each major goal your best efforts, and then be satisfied with what you have done. Don't punish yourself for falling short of perfection.

If you feel out of balance, check your schedule and review your priorities. Try to remove any items that do not coincide with your core values, as long as the change will not affect any of those values. For example, if you are miserable at your job because the hours do not allow you adequate time off to rest, you can't just quit and go home to sleep. You must analyze the situation and look for ways to reduce your hours and still pay your bills. Many times we get out of balance due to a concern over money so maintaining a budget and being able to save a little each paycheck for a rainy day is critical. Expect the best but plan for the worst. This way you can be ready for anything that life throws at you.

Maintaining Balance

Maintaining balance in your life is a continuous process. Your priorities will shift and change over time so don't get stuck in your ways. Continually evaluate where you are spending your time and who needs you the most. If there is a promotion coming up at work, it may be advantageous for you to spend more time there so that you can make more money and provide a better life for your family. However, be careful of getting stuck in a cycle where you are expected to work those hours all the time. Respectively, if there is an issue at home that needs your attention, explain it to your boss and temporarily focus more time there. If you are a good employee and the personal issues are few and far between, your boss should understand. Assess your situation every few months to make sure you are still on track toward achieving your goals. Update your time log a few times each year so that you can clearly see where you are spending time and where you may be wasting time. Always look for ways to complete tasks optimally so that you will have more free time to focus on tasks that you care about and enjoy.

Always be ready to adjust your balance and your focus as needed depending on the time and place. For example, things might be very stressful at work and you might interact with aggressive people who are hyper critical all day. However, when you get home, adjust your focus so that you are not on the attack or the defense. Certain behavior that may be acceptable in one situation may not be in another. Learn to fully be the person you need to be in the moment. If you are at work, be fully engaged in the work. If you are at home with your kids, be fully engaged in caring for them. Remember, keeping balance is an ongoing process and the balance for you is unique. Don't look at others and expect to be just like them. We are all distinct people and our priorities and obligations vary.

Conclusion

Although there is no easy formula for maintaining work/life balance, we can all make improvements to the balance we have now. We first need to know what our top priorities are and make plans to dedicate quality time to the things that matter most. Our ultimate goal should be to experience both achievement and fulfillment in every aspect of our lives. It is difficult to do this because we all have different obligations, but having balance is critical toward living a well-rounded life with passion and purpose. In order to thoroughly determine your true balance, maintain a time log that shows exactly where you are spending your time and then see if the number of hours matches to the priorities in your life. If there are areas that do not match, then you should make some changes.

There are a lot of tips and tools we can use to help us find our balance. Creating a schedule for both our professional and personal lives is a great first step. This allows for structure and consistency. Then share that schedule with others in your life and set up boundaries. Make sure people know when they can contact you and when they can not. Also, don't be afraid to say "no" if you are asked to perform a task you can not handle. Once you have this initial structure, compartmentalize the tasks you perform. When you are at work, be very focused at work. When you are home, focus exclusively on your personal life. This allows you to get more done. Then the next step is to reduce the waste and clutter in your life. If you do not have to perform a task that you no longer enjoy, then give it up. Then make sure to schedule fun activities and private time. It takes a lot of initiative to set up all of this structure, but the possible rewards are tremendous. Now that you have various tips and tools to enhance both your work life and personal life, the next and final step is to keep your sanity over time and build on your momentum of creating a fabulous life.

Ch. 10 – Keep Your Sanity Over Time

Your work is to discover your world and then with all your heart give yourself to it. --Buddha

This book is meant to inspire you to achieve better things for yourself and to truly enjoy the journey. If you follow the principles in this book and try the exercises, you can learn to love your job. You can also make your boss and co-workers happier too. You need to ask yourself what kind of mark you are leaving on this world. Is it a better place because you were here? If not, make an effort to contribute more and be a success. If you are not willing to make that effort, not only for yourself but for others too, then your life probably will not change much. On the other hand, if you are willing to try, the possible rewards are limitless.

Imagine what your future will be like if you achieve all of your hopes and dreams. What would you attempt to do if you could not fail? What kind of life would you like to lead? When you clearly write your hope and dreams down on paper, you have already increased their chances of coming true. Then completely imagine every detail of what it will feel like when they come to fruition. If you can envision these accomplishments so clearly, then you will be even further motivated to work toward them. Make sure to celebrate each milestone and reward yourself in the process. This will also help to keep your momentum.

Review

Hopefully you completed the assessments throughout this book and learned more about yourself and your particular work environment. The first chapter delved into the problems you are having at work and allowed you a chance to analyze those problems further. It also offered an overall job satisfaction assessment. By listing all of the major categories together in this one format, you can make contrasts and comparisons. Then you were able to proceed with the rest of the book and be aware of areas that may be strengths or particular areas that need improvement.

The second chapter was about getting organized, both physically and mentally. It provided tips for cleaning your work space, creating operator's manuals, and maintaining To-Do lists and status reports. These are important first steps in learning to love your job because sometimes we just can not see beyond the clutter in our lives. Getting organized allows us to see more clearly, which is necessary before we can move forward.

The third chapter was about setting goals and rewarding yourself. It is important to approach your job with purpose and to understand how your role fits in with the company mission. This involves understanding your own strengths and weaknesses and continually making improvements to expand your job description. In order to move forward, it is important to set clear goals. This chapter allowed you to create a personalized goal plan and to start planning the ways you will reward yourself.

The fourth chapter was about having a positive attitude and trying to spread that kind of energy to others. There are so many benefits to having a positive attitude and you are in total control of how you feel. This chapter described the different ways people are motivated and how negative scripts can weaken your ability to make progress in life. We also reviewed common pitfalls that cause negativity and how to deal with negative people.

The fifth chapter was about effective communication in its various forms. This included verbal and non-verbal skills, written communication, and the importance of listening. Different communication styles are needed at different times. Good communicators know how to read the situation and even how to read between the lines. We also communicate when we give presentations or when we host or attend meetings. Doing these things well can be extremely beneficial for your future career potential, especially if you want to work in management.

The sixth chapter was about building an alliance with your boss. This includes finding out what kind of person they are and how they prefer to interact with people. Using positive reinforcement is a great way to foster this relationship. It is also important to remember that they are human and will make mistakes but our goal it to manage their expectations of us while making every attempt to make them look good. This chapter offered tips on managing their expectations and filtering the information they receive.

The seventh chapter was about teambuilding and getting along with co-workers. Being part of a team means that you do not have to do all the work yourself. Being a good team member is advantageous to your reputation and to your career. This chapter provided basic tips for teamwork which include: being cooperative, being responsible, treating others the way they want to be treated, not keeping score, and embracing different viewpoints. This chapter also provided fun ideas that anyone can implement to make the work day more enjoyable.

The eighth chapter was about stress and the various symptoms and situations associated with it. Chronic stress can cause a myriad of health issues so it is critical to have knowledge on this topic. It is important for you to know what specifically stresses you out and how your body reacts to it. Then you can implement both proactive and reactive measures for combating stress. This chapter allowed you to further evaluate the specific stressors in your life and to begin creating a detailed action plan for addressing and reducing stress.

The ninth chapter was about maintaining work/life balance. We all lead unique lives so there is no template formula for staying in balance. A great place to start is by keeping a time log to see where you are actually spending your time. Then you can evaluate if you are spending it wisely on things that matter most. Five tools you can implement to be more in balance include: creating a schedule, setting boundaries, compartmentalizing the tasks you perform, reducing clutter and waste, and making time for yourself. If you get out of balance, remember your core values and always ask for help if you need it.

The topics in these chapters were chosen to present a comprehensive presentation of the skills needed to be a productive and happy employee in most job environments. The goals were to: learn more about yourself and your environment, learn to cultivate and promote a professional image, and learn to foster even better relationships with others. Each workplace is complex and requires a variety of skills just to get through the day. By understanding and implementing the techniques throughout this book, you can be more successful at your job and you can *learn to love it*.

Your Plan

This final exercise in important in order to summarize everything you learned. You will have a better chance of incorporating your plans if you actually write them down now.

List the top three things you learned by reading this book:

1.

2.

3.

List the top three changes or new initiatives you plan to incorporate into your job:

1.

2.

3.

Final Conclusion

Employees want to feel useful, appreciated, challenged, and have opportunities for advancement. Being happy and fulfilled in your job is one of the most rewarding experiences that you can have in life. People who feel this way look forward to going to work, they understand their role and how it fits into the overall success of the company, they are intrinsically motivated, and they have an optimistic outlook for their future career. Anyone can feel this way because we are each in control of our own emotions and desires. Remember, every morning you have a choice about how you are going to spend your day. You can make a conscious choice to be happy and plan for future career success, or you can spend your time being unhappy and stuck in a rut that will never change. The choice is yours but the time and effort required is the same. Hopefully you will always expect the best from yourself and from those around you. It is the only way to live.